THE EGYPTIAN GODS

By the Same Author

AN INTRODUCTION TO EGYPTIAN RELIGION

THE EGYPTIAN GODS

A Handbook

By

ALAN W. SHORTER, M.A. (Oxon)

*Assistant Keeper in the Department of Egyptian and
Assyrian Antiquities, British Museum.*

ROUTLEDGE & KEGAN PAUL
LONDON, HENLEY AND BOSTON

First published in 1937 by
Routledge & Kegan Paul Ltd
39 Store Street
London. WC1E 7DD,
Broadway House, Newtown Road
Henley-on-Thames
Oxon. RG9 1EN and
9 Park Street
Boston, Mass. 02108, USA
Reprinted in 1978
Printed in Great Britain by
Lowe & Brydone Ltd
Thetford, Norfolk

ISBN 0 7100 0037 5

CONTENTS

LIST OF PLATES

Between pages 62 and 63

PREFACE

This little book is intended as a guide for all who are interested in the <u>ancient Egyptian</u> religion. The gods figure so largely upon Egyptian monuments that the study of them may truthfully be said to occupy at least one half of Egyptology. But unfortunately these deities are so numerous, their relations with each other so complicated, and their external forms so confusing that the layman is often bewildered and discouraged. The present work, therefore, aims at providing the traveller in Egypt, or the visitor to Egyptian collections in museums, with a handbook in which he may find the most important facts concerning the Egyptian gods and the beliefs which surrounded them, presented as straightforwardly as possible. In endeavouring to do this the Author has obeyed the principal that the actual writings of the Egyptians themselves deserve premier consideration, and he has therefore given copious quotations from Egyptian religious texts, these quotations being printed in italics so that they may be easily consulted. It should also be pointed out that the book, as its title indicates, confines itself, as far as possible, to a consideration of the gods alone, and only briefly refers to other phenomena of religion in Egypt. Further, a Descriptive List of the Principal Egyptian Gods, in alphabetical order, has been added at the end of the book, which should enable the reader to recognize a good many upon the monuments for himself. Since, in this list, references are also given to the pages of the book on which the various gods are mentioned, a separate index has been considered unnecessary. The confusion which is to be observed in Egyptological books regarding the transliteration into English letters of Egyptian proper names has led the Author to employ, with occasional exceptions, a slightly modified form of the system regularly used by the late Sir E. A. Wallis Budge. For books of a non-technical nature this system still remains, in the Author's opinion, the most convenient, and it is used here for that reason only. Other transliterations of names, however, which will be found in many books, are added in brackets in the Descriptive List of gods.

My sincere thanks are due to my Wife for helpful criticisms, and to the authorities of the Egyptian Museum, Cairo, the Louvre, Paris, and the Musées Royaux, Brussels, for permission to reproduce illustrations of objects in their collections, also to the Oriental Institute of the University of Chicago, jointly with the Egypt Exploration Society, for allowing me to reproduce the picture of Horus in Plate I.

A. W. SHORTER.

CARSHALTON,
April, 1937.

To the Memory of H. R. Hall

TABLE OF EGYPTIAN HISTORY

Prehistoric or Predynastic Period.

Archaic Period (Dynasties I–III), beginning about 3300 B.C.

Old Kingdom or Pyramid Age (Dynasties IV–VI), beginning about 2900 B.C.

First Intermediate Period (Dynasties VII–X), beginning about 2400 B.C.

XIth Dynasty. Middle Kingdom.

XIIth Dynasty, about 2000 B.C. Middle Kingdom.

Dynasties XIII–XIV. Middle Kingdom.

Hyksos Period (Dynasties XV–XVI), about 1788–1580 B.C.

XVIIth Dynasty.

XVIIIth Dynasty (First Empire), about 1580–1321 B.C. New Kingdom.

XIXth Dynasty, about 1321–1205 B.C. Second Empire. New Kingdom.

XXth Dynasty, about 1205–1100 B.C. Second Empire. New Kingdom.

XXIst Dynasty (The Priest-Kings), about 1100–950 B.C. New Kingdom.

XXIInd Dynasty (Libyans), about 947–720 B.C. New Kingdom.

XXVth Dynasty (Ethiopians), about 745–650 (?) B.C. Late Period.

XXVIth Dynasty (Renaissance), 663–525 B.C. Late
    Period.

Conquest of Egypt by the Persians under Cambyses,
    525 B.C. Late Period.

Last Native King of Egypt, Nekhtherheb, 359–
    342 B.C. Late Period.

Alexander the Great takes possession of Egypt,
    332 B.C.

The Ptolemies (XXXIIIrd Dynasty), 305–30 B.C.

After the death of Antony and Cleopatra Egypt
    becomes a Roman Province, 30 B.C.

Roman Period, 30 B.C.–A.D. 640.

Arab Conquest, A.D. 640.

INTRODUCTION

AS in the case of most ancient peoples it is, strictly, impossible to speak of " the Egyptian religion ". In very early times, before 3300 B.C. when the historical age began, we find that each district in Egypt possessed its own special god or gods, and that, originally, the worship of these was more or less confined to the localities in question. During the Predynastic period, however, as first one township and then another so grew in power and influence that they were able to extend their rule over surrounding communities, the influence of the local gods likewise developed, with the natural result that certain deities rose head and shoulders above their fellows, and acquired an increasingly popular cult. The same is true of the historic age, which began with the unification of Upper and Lower Egypt by Menes, the founder of the First Dynasty of Kings, only by that time the religious systems of the various gods had already, to a large extent, become intermingled, this deity had been identified, for practical reasons, with that, and we are faced with the difficult problem of disentangling various cults which had once been distinct. During the three thousand years of Egyptian history which followed the same processes were at work. When the royal power is held by this or that family, we find that the god of the place from which the reigning house came enjoys an increased influence. But the struggle is now more or less confined to a limited number of important gods, and their cults soon command such widespread acceptance that, for the purpose of this book, they may be taken as together making up " the Egyptian religion ".

During the period of the Eighteenth and Nineteenth Dynasties (about 1580–1205 B.C.), Egypt reached the zenith of her civilization. The Pharaohs ruled over an empire which stretched through Palestine and Syria in the north as far as the Euphrates, and in the south to the fourth cataract of the Nile in the Sudan. At no other time was the economic prosperity of the country greater, and the vast riches drawn by the Pharaohs from their dominions were largely expended in religious endowments of various kinds, especially in erecting those magnificent temples which are the admiration of the world to-day. During the period of the New Kingdom (about 1580–900 B.C.), the Egyptian gods enjoyed their greatest splendour, and, owing to the wealth of the material, we are able to form a more complete picture of them at this time than at any other. To present this picture as clearly as possible is the aim of this little book. In the following pages, therefore, disputed questions of religious origins and the early histories of the different cults will only occasionally be mentioned. But the reader will be able to use the information given here as a basis for more detailed study in the larger works listed on page 144.

CHAPTER I

THE SUN-GOD—THE CREATION—THE GREAT GODS—ÁMEN, GOD OF THEBES

In certain countries the phenomenon of nature which dominates all others is the sun. Not only do its brilliancy and heat demand respect, but it is also the giver of life, the ripener of the crops sown by man. It is not surprising, therefore, to find that the Egyptians, like other primitive peoples, worshipped the sun as a god, or that they went further and regarded him as the principal god, the creator of the universe, the source of all life. The home of the Sun-god's cult was Heliopolis, a few miles north-east of modern Cairo; but at an early period in Egyptian history his influence had spread over the whole country, with the result that not only was every local god identified in some way with the Sun-god, but the ritual of most Egyptian temples was based upon the liturgy celebrated in the Sun-temple at Heliopolis. The god is represented in Egyptian art under several forms and names. In human form he is called Átum, and wears upon his head the double crown of Egypt, the combination of the red crown of Lower Egypt and the white crown of Upper Egypt worn by Pharaoh. A second

4

and very important form was that of Kheprâ, the sacred scarab beetle. This beetle is accustomed to collect a ball of dung for food, and to roll it between its legs until it can dig a cavity in the ground wherein to devour it. The Egyptians, confusing this food-ball with the pear-shaped ball of dung in which the female lays her egg, and which she buries in the earth till hatching-time, saw in the scarab-beetle a symbol of the Sun-god, who every day rolled the ball of the sun across the sky from east to west. A living beetle came from the dung pellet, apparently self-created ; life also came because of the sun, and the Sun-god, as Creator of all things, like the scarab was *self-created*. But the form in which the Sun-god most usually appears is that of a man with the head of a falcon, surmounted by the solar disc and cobra (the *uraeus*-serpent). In this form he is called Râ, his most frequent name, and he owes the falcon's head to identification with Horus,[1] another solar god who was worshipped in various parts of Egypt from early times. Equated with Horus he is often called Râ-Ḥerakhty, i.e. "*Râ-Horus the horizon-dweller*".

Every morning at dawn Râ appeared from behind *Manu*, the mountain of sunrise, and sailed across the sky in his *boat of millions of years*, accompanied by the gods of his train. The scene is well described in certain hymns composed in honour of the god :—

---

[1] Not to be confused with Horus, son of Osiris.

*Hail thou, Ḥerakhty-Kheprà, the self-created !
How beautiful is thy dawning in the horizon, when
thou illuminest the two Lands with thy beams !
All the gods rejoice when they behold thee as King
of all the sky. The uraeus-serpent is fixed on thy
head, the crowns of Upper and Lower Egypt on thy
brow. . . . Thōth stands at the prow of thy boat,
smiting all thine enemies.*[1]

Again :

*I have seen Horus at the helm and Thōth acting
at his command. I have taken hold of the prow-rope
of the Mesektet-boat and the stern-rope of the
Mānjet-boat.*[2]

It was thought by some that Rā aged during the
day. At dawn he was a new-born child, by midday
he was a hero in the prime of life, and at sunset he
became an old man tottering with feeble steps into
the western horizon. The god made use of two
boats, which are mentioned in the text quoted above.
During the day he crossed the sky in the *Mānjet*-
boat, but at evening he embarked on a second ship
called *Mesektet* for his night-voyage. This journey
lay through the regions of the Underworld and will
be described in Chapter IV.

At the beginning of time, when as yet neither
earth, sky, gods or men had been created, the Sun-
god existed alone in the watery mass of *Nūn* which

[1] *Book of the Dead.* Papyrus of Ani. Sheet 20.
[2] Ibid. Sheet 1.

illed the universe : *I am Átum when he was alone
in Nūn, I am Rā when he dawned, when he began to
rule that which he had made.*[1] By having sexual
union with himself the Sun-god created two other
deities whom he spat out of his mouth, the god
Shu, personification of air, and the goddess Tefnūt,
personification of moisture. These in turn produced
two children, Geb the earth-god and Nūt the goddess
of the sky, and, finally, from Geb and Nūt sprang
four children, Osiris and his consort Isis, Sēth and
his consort Nephthys.

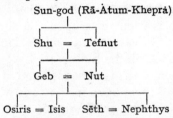

Sun-god (Rā-Átum-Kheprá)

Shu = Tefnut

Geb = Nut

Osiris = Isis   Sēth = Nephthys

These nine gods together made up the *Great Ennead*
(or *Nine*) of Heliopolis, the most important body of
gods in the Egyptian pantheon.

At first Geb and Nūt were locked together in an
embrace, but Shu came between them and tore them
apart, raising up Nūt to become the sky, and leaving
Geb, the earth, lying prostrate beneath her. The
sky was thus pictured as a goddess of colossal size
stooping over the world, her head being in the
west, and her thighs, between which Rā was reborn

[1] *Book of the Dead.* Spell 17, Section 1.

daily, in the east. Alternatively the sky was thought of as a huge cow, the goddess Meḥt-urt, along whose belly the Sun-god proceeded in his boat. According to another story the first portion of the earth to come into being was a small hill of land which the Sun-god summoned up out of the watery mass of Nūn, and on which he took his stand. The creation of mankind, as distinct from that of the gods, was accounted for in different ways. According to one legend the Sun-god is made to say : *I gathered together my limbs and wept upon them, and mankind came into being from the tears which flowed from mine eye.*[1] This explanation rests upon the similarity of the words *remyt* " tears " and *remeth* " mankind ". Other versions attribute the creation of men and women to Khnemu, the ram-headed god of Elephantine, who formed them upon his potter's wheel, or to Ptaḥ of Memphis, the artificer-god.

But even as, in the book of Genesis, God saw that the deeds of men were evil and resolved to destroy them from the face of the earth, so Rā became wroth with mankind whom he had created. For men began to murmur against him saying : *Lo, His Majesty (may he live, prosper and be healthy!) is grown old. His bones are silver, his flesh gold and his hair real lapis lazuli!*[2] This complaint was heard by the

---

[1] Legend of Creation in Brit. Mus. papyrus No. 10188.
[2] Legend of the Destruction of Mankind, inscribed on a wall in the tomb of Seti I.

myth

Sun-god, who was so enraged that he summoned a council of the gods and declared to them his intention of destroying his rebellious creatures. His own Eye (i.e. the sun itself), therefore, in the form of the goddess Hathor, was sent against them, and wrought such fearful slaughter that the land was drenched in blood. The Sun-god was now appeased by this punishment, but unfortunately could not persuade Hathor to cease from her butchery ! He had, in consequence, to resort to a ruse if the rest of mankind was to be preserved. At his order the gods brewed seven thousand vessels of an especially potent beer, in which they mixed a red colouring matter so that it would resemble blood, and emptied it out over the earth. *Then this goddess came in the early morning. She found these fields flooded, and her face was mirrored beautifully therein. So she drank, and her heart was glad, and she became drunken, and did not recognize mankind.*[1]

Unhappily the Sun-god's troubles were not confined to his dealings with men, for even his own eye (i.e. the sun itself) rebelled against him. The eye had wandered away for some reason, and had to be brought back by the god Thōth. But on its return it was enraged to find that another eye (i.e. the moon, or the night-sun as opposed to the sun of day ?) had been set in its place. In the Sun-god's own words *it raged at me after it had come and found*

[1] Ibid.

that I had made another eye in its place.[1] However, *it was Thōth who pacified it after it had fallen into a rage,*[2] and the Sun-god appeased it by making a place for it in his face.

In early times, when the cults of the various Egyptian gods were distinct from one another, several deities, besides the Sun-god, were regarded by their respective worshippers as having created the universe. The most important of these was Ptaḥ of Memphis, a god whose pictures and statues suggest that he was originally a primitive idol carved out of a stock of wood. During the later period of which we are writing Ptaḥ was believed, like other gods who had once been independent, to have exercised his creative functions at the command of the Sun-god, but an ancient text preserved in the British Museum [3] tells a different story. In this text it is stated that Ptaḥ was actually the creator of the Sun-god, who first came into existence as a thought conceived in his heart which then found utterance upon his tongue. Not only did Ptaḥ create gods, men and the whole universe ; as the divine artificer he made the very cult-images of gods which were worshipped in the temples.

He fashioned the gods, he made towns, he founded nomes, he set the gods in their seats of worship, he

---

[1] Brit. Mus. papyrus No. 10188.
[2] *Book of the Dead.* Spell 167.
[3] Stela No. 498.

established their bread-offerings, he founded their
chapels, and he made their bodies like what was
pleasing to their hearts. So the gods entered into
their bodies of all kinds of wood, all kinds of mineral,
all kinds of clay, and of all other things which grow
upon him in which they have taken form.

In this capacity of artificer Ptaḥ was worshipped
as the patron of all arts and crafts, and his High-
priest accordingly bore the title *Chief of the Master-*
workmen. It is not surprising, therefore, that in
later times Ptaḥ was identified by the Greeks with
Hephaistos and by the Romans with Vulcan. The
goddess who was worshipped at Memphis as the
consort of Ptaḥ was the fierce Sekhmet, with the
head of a lioness, and the Memphite triad was completed by their son Nefertem, a god who wears upon
his head a lotus bloom from which two tall plumes
rise. Sekhmet was identified by theologians
with the Sun-god's eye in its dangerous form (see
the legend of the Destruction of Mankind quoted
above), while Nefertem was regarded as the lotus
which he held to his nose.

Returning to our consideration of the Sun-god,
we find that, to the ordinary Egyptian, the god's
most important aspect was that connected with
the King. The Egyptian Pharaoh was believed to
be both the physical son and the earthly embodiment
of Rā. This is clearly shown by the official titles
assumed by the monarch and by the insignia which

he wore. He was called *Son of Rā* and *bodily son of Rā*, and was said to be *endowed with life, stability and well-being like Rā forever*. The names of Kings, written within an oval which is termed the " cartouche ", are frequently compounded with that of the Sun-god, e.g. *Neb-Maāt-Rā* = Lord-of-Truth-is-Rā (Åmenḥetep III); *Men-Maāt-Rā* = Abider-in-Truth-is-Rā (Seti I). On his forehead, its hood extended and its body twisting back over the crown of his head, Pharaoh wore the golden *uraeus*-cobra , the special emblem of the Sun-god, which, in the hyperbole of Egyptian texts, is described as spitting fire against the enemy when the King fought in battle. When Pharaoh died he rejoined his divine father in the sky, where he reigned with him in glory. Thus the death of Åmenemḥat I, founder of the Twelfth Dynasty, is described in these words :

> *In the thirtieth year, on the seventh day of the third month of Inundation, the god entered his horizon. The King of Upper and Lower Egypt Seḥetep-āb-Rā flew to the sky and was united with the sun, the body of the god was merged with him who made him.*[1]

· It may be seen, therefore, that the Sun-god is rightly considered to have been the most important of the Egyptian gods, and he remained such throughout Egyptian history. It might happen that political

[1] From a literary composition known as the " Story of Sinuhe ".

developments gave prominence to some other deity for a time, but always the solar theology exerted its influence in the background, modifying all other systems to suit itself. Even Osiris (who will be discussed in Chapter III), the Sun-god's most deadly rival, became solarized, and his system was adapted to that of Heliopolis. (At the moment, however, we must turn to consider the god who, of all the members of the Egyptian pantheon, played the most spectacular part during the imperial age of the New Kingdom, Ámen of Thebes.)

The principal shrine of Ámen was at Thebes in Upper Egypt, and, consequently, during the first great period of Egyptian history, known as the Old Kingdom, he did not play a leading part. When, however, the throne passed to a family coming from Thebes, the Pharaohs of the Middle Kingdom, the local god obtained a greater prominence. Later still, when the Theban princes of the Seventeenth Dynasty succeeded in throwing off the hated yoke of the Hyksōs, the foreigners who had invaded the country at the collapse of the Middle Kingdom, they saw in Ámen the giver of their victory. From that moment his influence steadily grew, until, when Egypt had achieved her empire in Asia and the Sudan, Ámen became the very symbol of her might.

It is thought by some that Ámen (Plate 2) was originally a deity representing air and wind, the cosmic element which first created life amid the inert chaos which had prevailed before the universe was fashioned. Later on he possessed the characteristics of a god, Min, the centre of whose worship was at the cities of Panopolis and Coptos, and like him is usually depicted as a man wearing a head-dress from which rise two tall plumes, and sometimes, also like that god, standing with sexual member erect (thus emphasizing his generative powers) and right hand raised, holding a sceptre in the form of a whip. But no deity who aspired to the position of State God could hope for success unless he harmonized with the great body of solar doctrine on which the Egyptian Kingship was based. It was necessary, therefore, for the priesthood of Åmen to identify him with the Sun-god, and so he became Åmen-Rā, the whole of solar doctrine was applied to him, and he was thenceforward regarded as identical in every way with Rā himself. A hymn describes him as :

> *More exalted of nature than any other god, at whose beauty the gods rejoice. He to whom praise is given in the Great House, who is crowned in the House of Fire. He whose sweet savour the gods love, when he cometh from Punt.*[1] *Richly perfumed when he cometh from the land of the Mejayu.*[1] *Fair of face when he cometh from the land* [1] *of the god.*[2]

As the Sun-god he was believed to be the physical

---

[1] Lands of incense and fragrant gums.
[2] From a papyrus in the Cairo Museum.

father of every Pharaoh, who, as his heir, received the throne from his hands. In order to beget his heir Åmen would assume the outward appearance of the reigning Pharaoh and visit the Queen while she slept in her palace.

He found her as she rested in the beauty of her palace. She awoke at the perfume of the god and laughed in presence of his Majesty. He straightway came unto her and greatly desired her, he gave his heart to her, and he caused her to behold him in his divine form after he had come into her presence. She rejoiced to behold his beauty and his love passed into her body; the palace overflowed with the perfume of the god, and all his savour was that of Punt.[1]

But at this time of imperial expansion Åmen stood to the Egyptians even more for a god of victory, a war-lord who inspired Pharaoh his son to prosecute the campaigns which would bring all nations under his sway, and make them in a very real sense tributaries of him as well as of the earthly king. The reliefs carved upon the walls of temples frequently show the victorious Pharaoh sacrificing prisoners of war in the god's presence, dashing out their brains with a stone-headed mace, or leading captive chieftains before him. Addressing Thothmes III Åmen says :

[1] Inscription in the temple of Ḥatshepsut at Dĕr el-baḥri.

> *I have come that I may cause thee to tread down the princes of Palestine ;*
> *I spread them out beneath thy feet throughout their countries.*
> *I cause them to behold thy majesty as the Lord of Radiance,*
> *Thou shinest in their faces as mine image.*[1]

When Rameses II, in his war against the Hittites, is cut off and surrounded by the enemy at the battle of Kadesh, he cries out to Åmen in his hour of need and the god replies : *On, on! I, thy father, am with thee! My hand is with thee, and I am of more avail than an hundred thousand men! I the lord of victory, lover of strength!* [2] Whereupon the hard-pressed Pharaoh regains his courage and launches such a vigorous attack upon the foe that they are driven into the river by the force of his charge. *I am like Menthu!* he cries, *I shoot on the right hand and fight on the left! I am before thee like Baal in his hour! I find that the two thousand five hundred chariots, in whose midst I was, lie cut to pieces before my steeds!* [2]

Åmen was worshipped in conjunction with two other deities, who with him made up the divine triad of Thebes. These were his consort Mūt and

---

[1] From Thothmes' Stela of Victory, in the Cairo Museum.
[2] From a Poem describing the battle of Kadesh, preserved on a papyrus in the British Museum (Papyrus Sallier III), and on temple walls in Egypt.

their son Khensu. The goddess Mūt was originally a vulture goddess, and is sometimes depicted in the form of that bird, but she more usually appears in human form, as a woman wearing the Double Crown of Egypt upon her head. The god Khensu, however, was of a more complex nature. It is thought by some scholars that his name means *Placenta-of-the-King*, and that in origin he was actually what his name implies, the placenta being revered as the King's ghostly twin, with which the King's existence was mysteriously bound up. At any rate Khensu is frequently represented in art as a handsome young prince, as in an exceedingly beautiful statue of him found at Karnak, belonging to the end of the Eighteenth Dynasty, which is now in the Cairo Museum (No. 38,488). In this statue he wears upon his head a tight-fitting cap, from the front of which rises the *uraeus*-snake, symbol of royalty. Upon his right shoulder falls the side-lock of plaited hair worn by young princes, and on his chin is the stiff beard peculiar to gods. The kingly nature of Khensu is further demonstrated by the whip and shepherd's crook held in his hands, both of which were insignia of the King since early times. Round the god's neck, over his flat bead collar, hangs a necklace known as the *menât*, an object which was at once an ornament and a sacred rattle, possessing magical power. In addition to the crook and whip he holds before him a sceptre compounded of three common symbols, ☥ *ānkh*, signifying " life ", ☦ *tet*, signifying " stability " or " duration ", and the *uas* ⌐, a sceptre often carried by gods. On his head Khensu generally wears the full disc of the moon within the crescent, since he was also regarded as a moon-god, and this is his headdress even when he is represented with a falcon's head, which he had acquired in the usual process of solarization to which most Egyptian gods were subjected at one time or another. To these three gods, *Åmen-Rā, King of the gods, lord of Karnak, Mūt the great, lady of Åsher*, and *Khensu in Thebes, Nefer-ḥetep*, the most splendid temples of ancient Egypt were raised, and they will be described in the following chapter.

Chapter II

AN EGYPTIAN TEMPLE—THE TEMPLES OF THEBES—THE GODS OF THE COMMON PEOPLE

(A typical Egyptian temple of the New Kingdom will be first described, since this form was preserved unaltered down to the end of Egyptian history ; although there was often multiplication of individual parts the general scheme remained the same. The temple is approached by an avenue flanked by ram-sphinxes, and entered by a massive wooden door set between two great towers. These towers, which we call " pylons ", give almost the appearance of a fortification, and, set up in great slots let into their outer face, rise tall flag-staves made of wood from Lebanon, from the top of which flutter bright-coloured pennons. In the thickness of the pylons are staircases leading up to their flat roofs, and the inner and outer faces of the towers, which are given a pronounced " batter ", are carved with huge reliefs of Pharaoh smiting his enemies with uplifted mace.

Within the temple precincts we find ourselves standing in an open court surrounded by a colonnaded porch, the columns being shaped and brilliantly coloured to represent either lotus or papyrus plants growing out of the water. From the court a few shallow steps lead to the transverse columned hall known as the " hypostyle ", dimly lighted by clerestory windows, and thence we pass to the sanctuary itself, which consists of a single chamber in which stands the god's shrine. The shrine is made either of stone [1] or wood, but in either case is closed by two folding wooden doors, bolted and sealed with a clay seal. Within the shrine is kept the cultus-image of the god, a figure which is not more than about two or three feet high, made of solid gold, or of costly wood overlaid with gold leaf, and inlaid with semi-precious stones. An early example (Sixth Dynasty) of what may have been such a cultus-image is preserved in the Cairo Museum. It was found in the temple at Hieraconpolis, and is the head of the hawk-god Horus, wrought of gold, and intended to be fixed to a copper body. The workmanship is very fine, and the eyes of the bird are strikingly represented by a single rod of black obsidian which pierces the head from side to side, the ends only being visible. Instead of an upright shrine there would sometimes be a large model boat, made of wood overlaid with gold, resting upon a stone pedestal ; the image would then stand

[1] For a good example of the Ptolemaic period, see Brit. Mus. No. 1134, in the Egyptian Sculpture Gallery.

inside the boat's cabin, which was covered by a veil in order to cut off the gaze of the profane. This boat, containing the image of the god, was carried in procession out of the temple upon the shoulders of priests during great festivals.

Grouped around and behind the sanctuary is a number of other chambers, some of which were repositories of vestments and sacred utensils, while others are chapels dedicated to deities associated with the god of the temple. Thus, in a temple of Åmen there are generally chapels of Mūt and Khensu, and sometimes others dedicated to gods not so closely connected with him. For example, in the great temple built by Seti I at Abydos, there are seven sanctuaries; the central one is dedicated to Åmen-Rā, and the others to Osiris, Isis, Horus, Ḥerakhty, Ptaḥ, and Seti himself. The coloured reliefs which cover the walls and columns of a temple mainly depict processions at religious festivals, the King dedicating food-offerings or the spoil of foreign conquest to the gods, or scenes from his campaigns. The last mentioned are confined to the outer court, pylons and exterior walls, the scenes becoming purely religious as we advance into the more sacred portions of the building. On entering the sanctuary we find that the reliefs and inscriptions there are concerned only with the ritual actually performed within it, and such reliefs, when taken in conjunction with copies of service-books preserved on papyrus,[1] are valuable evidence for the reconstruction of Egyptian temple-ritual.

The priesthood of a temple was divided into two main classes, the higher bearing the title *ḥem-neter*, meaning literally " god's servant ", usually rendered by scholars as " prophet ", the lower *uāb*, literally " the pure ". In addition to these there were " fathers of the god ", a rank not including the *uāb*-priests, and " lectors " (*khery-ḥeb*), who were classed with the *uāb*-priests. At the head of the whole temple staff was the *ḥem-neter tepy*, the " Chief Prophet " or " High-priest ". Priestesses were also attached to many of the temples, their duty being chiefly that of making music with their rattles (*sistra*) as an accompaniment to the services. In the case of Åmen, who was a god of markedly sexual character, these priestesses were regarded as concubines of the god, the High-priest's wife bearing the title of " Chief Concubine of Åmen ", while the queen of the reigning Pharaoh was thought of as being Åmen's ccnsort, and was accorded the title of " God's-wife of Åmen ". The temple staff was divided into four " gangs " or " courses " (in Egyptian *sa*), each of which served in turn for one lunar month. At the end of this period the outgoing course was accustomed to provide an inventory of the temple effects, which would be checked by the

---

[1] e.g. the rituals for the worship of Åmen and Mūt, now in the Berlin Museum.

incoming shift and declared correct. The main duties of the priesthood were the general care of the temple, and the celebration of the divine rites which we will now describe.

In the Egyptian theocracy the King was not only regarded as the head of the whole priesthood of Egypt, but was actually supposed to be the officiant at every temple-service. In reality this was impossible, but the fiction was kept up in the sculptures covering the walls of a temple, in which the Pharaoh appears as officiant in all the divine rites. In actual fact, naturally, his place was taken by the High-priest or another cleric of the temple in question, unless some great festival was in progress at which Pharaoh himself was present. The ritual employed in most temples was based, as we have already said, upon that which had been used in the temple of the Sun-god at Heliopolis from very early times, the form taken being that of the god's toilet, the cult-image being fumigated, washed, anointed, dressed, and finally presented with a meal. After the god had consumed the spiritual essence of the food, the material food which remained was divided among the priests. As reconstructed from a papyrus at Berlin (already mentioned), and from the temple sculptures, the liturgy of Ámen-Rā at Karnak proceeded as follows.

First the celebrant enters the sanctuary and kindles a light in his censer. The Egyptian censer was not of the swinging kind, but consisted of a long metal object shaped like a human arm, in the hand of which a small pottery vessel for the incense was fixed. Reciting the words of the liturgy, the celebrant advances towards the shrine containing the god's image, and when this initial purification of the sanctuary and of himself is completed, proceeds to break the string of papyrus and the clay seal which secure the bolts of the shrine doors. He then draws back the bolts, flings open the wooden doors and beholds his god face to face. *The two doors of the sky are opened!* he recites. *The two doors of earth are unclosed, Geb gives greeting, saying unto the gods who abide upon their seats :*

> " *Heaven is opened, the company of gods shines forth !*
> *Åmen-Rā, Lord of Karnak, is exalted upon his great seat !*
> *The Great Nine are exalted upon their seats !*
> *Thy beauties are thine, O Åmen-Rā, Lord of Karnak !* "

Overcome by the splendour of Åmen the celebrant falls down and, lying prone, *kisses the ground* before the shrine. Rising again he intones a hymn of praise, and then presents the statue with scented honey and fumigates it with incense. The preliminaries of the service are now completed, and, after taking the statue out of the shrine and standing it on a little pile of sand, the priest begins the most important section of the liturgy, the actual toilet of the god. First he washes the image with water from sacred vessels exclaiming : *Purified, purified is Åmen-Rā, Lord of Karnak ! Take to thee the water which is in the eye of Horus ; given to thee is thine eye, given to thee is thy head, given to thee are thy bones, established for thee is thy head upon thy bones in the presence of Geb !*

He again censes the image, and now puts a white head-cloth on its head and arrays it in other cloths of green and red, crowning it with its special diadem, placing sceptres in its hands, and bracelets and anklets upon its arms and legs. After this the statue is anointed with more unguent, and its eyelids are painted first with green and then with black cosmetics. The celebrant now replaces the statue in its shrine, and sets a liberal supply of food and drink on a table before it, burning yet more incense in his censer, probably in order that the spiritual essence of the meal may be conveyed to the god by means of the smoke. The liturgy is now finished, the doors of the shrine are bolted and sealed, and, after sweeping the floor to obliterate his own footprints, the celebrant leaves the sanctuary.

We have already referred to the great temples erected for Åmen, the State-god, at Thebes, and will now turn to consider them in detail, since they are in some ways the most impressive of all the monuments of Egyptian religion. The temple of which the Egyptian name was *House of Åmen in the Southern Ḥarīm*, stands to the south in the modern village of Luxor, and in ancient days was connected with the northern temples at Karnak by a road flanked by stone sphinxes. The most striking features of this temple to-day are the beautiful colonnaded court built by Åmenḥetep III, in which the columns represent bundles of lotus buds, and the huge colonnade which leads into it, mainly the work of Åmenḥetep III, but ornamented with reliefs by Tutānkhåmen and Ḥeremḥeb. These reliefs depict for us in great detail the most magnificent of the festivals of Åmen at Thebes, in which the King himself played a leading part. This was the Festival of *Åpt*, celebrated at the New Year, in which the costly barques of Åmen, his consort Mūt and his son Khensu were floated down the river to Luxor amid the rejoicings of the populace. The Temple of Luxor, however, is small in comparison with that of Karnak, which bore the name *Elect of Places*. The area of the enclosure surrounding the latter is over sixty-one acres, and it could find room within its walls for St. Peter's (Rome) together with the Cathedrals of Milan and Notre Dame (Paris). The temple is approached from a stone quay, once abutting on the Nile, which has now receded to a considerable distance, and the visitor walks up an avenue of ram-sphinxes to find himself standing before the great pylon gateway of the Ethiopian Kings, 370 feet wide, 142 feet high and 49 feet thick. Beyond this pylon lies the ruined First Court, erected mainly during the Twenty-second Dynasty, which could hold St. Paul's Cathedral (London) leaving nearly 10,000 square feet to spare. From this we pass through the second Pylon, of Rameses I, into the great Hypostyle Hall, the largest single chamber of any building in the world. It was erected mainly by Seti I of the Nineteenth Dynasty, although part of the decoration is the work of Rameses II. The twelve central columns of the hall, with capitals imitating the open papyrus flower, tower up to a height of 69 feet, the columns of the side aisles, in the form of clustered papyrus buds, to a height of 43 feet, and, when the roof was in place, the building was dimly lit by the light which filtered through the clerestory windows above the nave. The surface of the columns and walls is richly sculptured with scenes of Seti I and Rameses II offering to the gods and performing other religious functions, while the exterior walls are covered with great battle-pieces illustrating the campaigns of these two Pharaohs in Palestine and Syria.

Leaving the hall through the third pylon, of Amenḥetep III, and crossing the central court which lies beyond, we walk through the fourth pylon into the hall erected by Thothmes I. It was in this hall that there is said to have taken place one of those dramatic events in which the Egyptian gods intervened on behalf of a claimant to the throne, in this case the young prince who afterwards became Thothmes III, creator of the Egyptian empire. An inscription tells us that while he was still a stripling in the priesthood of Åmen's temple, and had not yet even been raised to the rank of prophet, his father, the Pharaoh Thothmes I, was officiating one day at an important service in this hall. Presently the image of the god, hidden in the cabin of his sacred boat, was borne forth from the sanctuary on the shoulders of the priests and began to make a circuit of the hall. Suddenly the boat stopped before the young priest and the god spoke to him, granting him in that very moment a vision in which he *flew up to the sky as a hawk* and was there solemnly crowned King by the Sun-god himself, receiving from him the various splendid epithets of his royal titulary. It is doubtful whether the incident recorded in this inscription ever really took place,[1] but if it did it was, no doubt, a cleverly staged *coup d'etat* arranged by the young Thothmes and the priests of Åmen.

When, however, Thothmes I died the reins of power were seized by his strong-willed daughter

[1] For a discussion of this question see my *Introduction to Egyptian Religion*, pp. 79 ff.

Ḥatshepsut, who, after the death of Thothmes II,
reigned for twenty-two years as *King*, while the
unfortunate Thothmes III had perforce to remain
in the background. During this period Ḥatshepsut
unroofed her father's hall and set up on its floor two
great obelisks, one of which to-day lies overthrown,
while the other still stands erect, a single block of
granite 76 feet in height. It was the custom to set up
these gigantic monoliths in large numbers within the
precincts of temples ; generally they stand in pairs
before a pylon, and in ancient times the pyramidions
on the top (and sometimes perhaps the whole
monument) were overlaid with gold or copper.
That they were symbols connected with the sun is
certain, but their exact origin has not been entirely
explained. The erection of Ḥatshepsut's obelisks
must be considered a masterpiece of engineering,
when it is remembered that these twin monoliths
had to be quarried at Assuān, 120 miles south
of Thebes, transported up the river to that city,
and there erected within the temple, and that the
inscription cut upon the base of the standing
monument informs us that the work of quarrying
occupied only seven months. Justly does Ḥatshepsut
proclaim the magnitude of her achievement in this
text, saying :

> *I declare unto the people who shall come to be
> after two æons, whose heart shall consider this
> monument which I have made for my father. . . .*

As I sat in the palace I remembered him who had created me, and my heart led me to make for him two obelisks of fine gold,[1] whose pyramidions should merge with the sky. . . .

O ye people who shall see my monument in future years, who shall speak of that which I have made, beware lest ye say : ' I know not, I know not why this was done, the fashioning of a mountain entirely of gold like something of usual occurrence ! ' I swear as Rā loves me, as my father Ámen praises me, as my nose is refreshed with life and well-being, as I assume the White Crown, as I appear in the Red Crown, as the Two Gods have united for me their portions, as I rule this land like the son of Isis, as I have waxed mighty like the son of Nūt, as Rā sets in the Evening-boat, as he endures in the Morning-Boat, as he consorts with his two mothers in the divine barque, as the sky abides, as that which he has made endures, as I shall exist unto eternity like an Imperishable Star, as I shall set in life like Átum, as for the two great obelisks which my Majesty has fashioned of fine gold for my father Ámen, in order that my name may abide and endure in this temple for ever and ever, they consist of a single block of hard red granite without join or mend !

Beyond the hall of Thothmes I lies a complex

---

[1] i.e. overlaid with gold.

of buildings which there is no space here to describe.
It includes the Hall of Records, inscribed with
excerpts from the official account of the campaigns
of Thothmes III ; the granite chapel erected by
Philip Arrhidæus (323–317 B.C.), the half-brother
of Alexander the Great, to take the place of the
old sanctuary ; the ruins of the Middle Kingdom
temple, and the Festival Hall of Thothmes III.
The last-mentioned hall was built in honour of the
Theban triad and in commemoration of the King's
many victories, and bore the name *Thothmes-is-
glorious-in-monuments*. It is remarkable for the
fact that its columns are shaped as tent-poles, and
one is irresistibly reminded of that other great
soldier, Napoleon Bonaparte, whose bedroom in the
palace of Malmaison imitates a military tent. To
the south-east of the great temple of Ámen lies the
sacred lake, on which his golden barque, *User-ḥat-
Ámen*, was floated on solemn occasions, and where,
according to a legend told by the natives of Karnak
to-day, it may still sometimes be seen at midnight,
its ghostly shape glittering in the light of the moon.
Further to the south, and connected with the temple
of Ámen by an avenue of sphinxes, may be found the
ruins of the temple of Mūt, *Lady of Ásher*, the consort
of Ámen, and to the south-west stands the temple
of their son Khensu, in excellent preservation, while
in other portions of the enclosure are small shrines
erected to Osiris, Ptaḥ and other gods. The visitor

who climbs the stairway of the Great Pylon, and views the gigantic ruins of Karnak from its summit, is well able to gauge the wealth which made the building and upkeep of these temples possible. In the reign of Rameses III, according to Papyrus Harris, which is preserved in the British Museum, the temples of Egypt owned nearly one-seventh of the cultivable land of the whole country, and of this the priesthood of Åmen had the largest share. Vast herds of cattle, and a huge personnel of officials, workmen and peasants, were assigned to them for the upkeep of the temple-estates. Gold, silver, and all kinds of precious material, the plunder of foreign campaigns and the harvest of yearly tribute from conquered peoples, were poured into their treasuries, while the Empire-builders even presented Åmen with whole districts in Syria and the Sudan to be a source of revenue. To the Egyptian of the New Kingdom the temple of Åmen at Karnak was the hub of the world, and its greatness a source of unending delight. *How glad is the temple of Åmen on New Year's day*, sing the musicians at a banquet . . . *when he receives its good things, and its oxen are slaughtered by hundreds, its wild game of the mountains by thousands, even for Åmen as his due offerings at the festivals of the seasons.* Åmen had become identified in the Egyptian mind with Egypt itself. He ruled in Karnak as king of the gods, creator of mankind and lord of the world, *Åmen-Rā the powerful, the divine lover, shining forth in Karnak his city, the lady of life.*

The contemplation of the great gods, however, such as Åmen-Rā, and of the magnificent temples in which their worship was conducted with elaborate ritual, leads us to inquire how much all this meant to the peasant-folk of ancient Egypt, who, like the *fellāḥīn* of to-day, formed the bulk of the population. It is certain that the common people were never at any time admitted to the worship which was carried on in the innermost halls and shrines of an Egyptian temple. At the most they were allowed as far as the first court on important festivals. Otherwise their only contact with the god must have been during an outdoor procession, when the image was carried in its sacred barque upon the shoulders of the priests. Popular devotion, however, to the great gods undoubtedly existed, as is proved by a number of private stelæ inscribed with prayers addressed to them, and by the large quantity of cheap votive figures of the gods which were dedicated in temples during the Late Period and Græco-Roman times. But there are indications that the uneducated masses often preferred to recommend themselves to the patronage of more homely deities, who would be more likely to take an interest in their humble interests and aspirations. Thus two creatures of hideous aspect but of a quite harmless character found a general acceptance in the

Egyptian home, namely, the god Bes and the goddess Taurt. Bes is depicted as a bandy-legged dwarf, his head sometimes surmounted by a row of feathers. He appears to have originally had the form of a lion or some other wild member of the cat tribe, for in many representations he has the ears, mane and tail of this creature, which are, however, often interpreted by the artist as a skin which he is wearing. This god was a great favourite, and countless pendants and amulets were made in his likeness. He was especially associated with human pleasures of every kind, and his genial figure adorns the foot of the marriage bed, or, beating a tambourine, he encourages his worshippers to sing and make merry. In the pictures carved on certain magical wands of ivory he is shown strangling and devouring serpents, in order to protect mankind from these noxious reptiles. The goddess Taurt was even more repulsive in form, being a curiously ingenious mixture of hippopotamus, lioness and crocodile, but her character was no less benevolent than that of Bes. Among other things she was closely associated with childbirth, a rôle which may possibly have been suggested by the appearance of pregnancy which her strange shape presents. The Egyptian craftsman produced charms in the form of this goddess in almost as large a quantity as of Bes.

In addition to these gods of universal popularity there were many of a purely local cult, genii who inhabited this or that sacred tree, or who dwelt in some particular rock or hill. A good example of such was the goddess " Peak-of-the-West ", who was worshipped at Thebes, and who is generally thought by Egyptologists to have been that spur of mountain on the west bank of the Nile opposite Luxor, which bears to-day the name of Sheikh 'Abd el-Ḳurna. " Peak-of-the-West " was sometimes identified with Isis, but was more usually regarded as the home of the serpent-goddess Mertseger who presided over the Theban Necropolis. A number of votive stelæ erected in honour of the Peak have been found, which show that she was inclined to be touchy and had to be treated with considerable respect. A stela now at Turin, erected by a certain employee of the necropolis called Nefer-ābu, tells how this ill-advised person *wrought the transgression against the Peak* and was severely punished in consequence. But eventually the goddess was merciful and forgave him, and so he addresses this solemn warning to others :

> *Mark, I will say to great and little among the workmen : Be ye ware of the Peak ! For a lion is within the Peak, who smites with the smiting of a savage lion and pursues him that transgresses against her.*

Even more attractive to the unlearned than hills and trees would be some living creature who had come to be regarded as the incarnation of a god or demon. Perhaps a half-wild cat would be seen slinking down a lonely *wādi*, or a bird had become tame enough to come day by day to some local shrine for crumbs. Thus a stela in the Turin Museum shows Nebrā, a draughtsman employed in the Theban necropolis, kneeling in adoration before a dove, while, in the lower section of the stela, his two sons Nekhtàmen and Khāy worship a cat. The latter is called, in the accompanying text, *the beautiful cat which endures, endures*, and the swallow, though in close proximity to its feline colleague, is termed with unconscious humour *the beautiful dove which endures, endures evermore*. Here, in the New Kingdom, we can observe the roots of that development of animal-worship which marked the Egyptian religion in its decline, and which was to culminate in the Græco-Roman period when the country became almost enslaved by an army of sacred cats, dogs, crocodiles, snakes, ibises, hawks and beetles, calling forth the ironic lines of Juvenal:

> *O sanctas gentes, quibus haec nascuntur in hortis Numina! . . .*

CHAPTER III

OSIRIS—JUDGMENT AFTER DEATH— IMMORTALITY

In the previous chapters we have considered all the more important Egyptian gods with the exception of one, perhaps the most important of all, Osiris, *King of eternity, ruler of everlastingness.* His cult, the original centre of which was the town of Busiris in the Delta, had existed from early times side by side with that of Rā the Sun-god, and was eventually to eclipse it in popularity. He seems to have been at first the personification of certain natural phenomena ; his continually repeated death and resurrection were manifested by the Nile as it yearly dwindled and swelled again to inundation, spreading over the fields its fertilizing mud. From this soil sprang the luxuriant crops and vegetation, and these, too, typified the dying and reviving god. As the ages passed Osiris drew under his influence other deities who originally were unconnected with him. Osiris himself was regarded as a beneficent king who had ruled over Egypt in prehistoric times. Sēth, god of Ombos, became his evil brother who murdered him ; Isis, the goddess of a town in the Delta, became his faithful consort, who by magical

power brought Osiris back to life ; Horus became
his son who avenged his father by defeating Sēth
in battle. Thus arose the legend which exerted a
more potent influence upon the minds of the
Egyptians than any other in their mythology, and
it will, therefore, be considered here at some length

The only connected version of the Osiris legend
preserved to us is that given by the late Greek writer
Plutarch, who lived in the First Century A.D.
According to him Osiris, when King of Egypt,
distinguished himself as a religious teacher, a framer
of laws, and an instructor of mankind in the arts
of agriculture, in all of which activities he was
ably seconded by his queen, the goddess Isis. Sēth,
however, who appears in the story under the Greek
name Typhon, formed a plot to remove Osiris and
seize the kingdom for himself, in which undertaking he secured the assistance of seventy-two
fellow-conspirators, and a certain Ethiopian queen
called Aso. Having contrived to obtain the measurements of his brother he ordered a beautifully
decorated chest of the same size to be made, and
brought it into the room in which Osiris was
banqueting. As if in jest Typhon declared that he
would give the chest to the person whose body would
be found to fit it, and Osiris himself was persuaded to
lie down inside. As soon as he was safely in the chest
the lid was fastened and secured with nails and
melted lead. The chest was then taken by the

murderers and cast into the Nile, which eventually bore it out to sea. The legend then proceeds to describe the wanderings of Isis, bereaved and lamenting, in search of her husband's body, and tells how she eventually discovered it at Byblos, whither the ocean had carried it. Returning to Egypt the goddess brought the chest with her, but it was soon found one night by Typhon when he was hunting by the light of the moon, and he tore the body of Osiris into fourteen pieces, scattering them in different places throughout the country. The long-suffering Isis was now forced to travel about Egypt searching for the remains, each of which she buried where she found it. Soon afterwards Osiris appeared from the Other World and encouraged his son Horus to avenge him, and the rest of the story describes how Horus, in a series of battles, utterly defeated Typhon, the murderer of his father, and presumably made himself King of Egypt.

Curiously enough nothing like a complete version of the Osiris legend has been preserved to us among the extensive remnant of Egyptian religious literature, but the texts are full of references to it, and frequently add details to the story. We learn, for instance, that at the death of Osiris Isis and her sister Nephthys changed themselves into two kites, which perched at his head and foot uttering cries of lamentation, and there are many accounts of how

Horus slew the companions of Sēth and inherited the throne of his father. For example, in Spell 1 of the Book of the Dead, the dead person, identifying himself with the god Thōth, is made to say : *O bull of the West* (i.e. Osiris), *I am the god of protection ! I have fought for thee. I am one of those gods of the council who justified Osiris against his enemies on that day of judgment. I belong to thy supporters, Osiris ! I am one of those gods, Children of Nūt, who slew the enemies of Osiris and imprisoned those who had rebelled against him. I belong to thy supporters, Horus ! I have fought for thee, I have pleaded for thy name. I am Thōth who justified Horus against his enemies on that day of judgment in the great House-of-the-Prince in Heliopolis.*

Besides the defeat of Sēth, the passage just quoted mentions two other events which form a sequel to the Osiris legend, and to which the Egyptian religious texts constantly refer. These are the trials of Osiris and Horus respectively before the great Nine of Heliopolis. Even after Horus had defeated Sēth in bloody conflict the arch-enemy had not yet played his last card. He arraigned his divine brother before the Nine of Heliopolis, the Sun-god acting as president of the council, on a number of charges of which the nature is not clearly known to us, but which were certainly directed against Osiris' claim to the throne of Egypt. As the Pyramid Texts tell us, Sēth lost his case : *The Two*

Truths heard (the case), Shu was witness. The Two Truths commanded that the thrones of Geb should revert to him (Osiris), that he should raise himself up to that which he desired, . . . that he should unite those who were in Nūn, and that he should bring to an end the words in Heliopolis.[1]

As a result of the trial, in which the cause of Osiris was pleaded by Thōth, Sēth was rejected and Osiris upheld. But even now Sēth had not finished, and he brought a second charge, this time against the youthful Horus, who claimed the throne of Egypt as the successor of his father Osiris. Sēth complained that Horus was illegitimate, a charge which is perhaps connected with the tradition that the latter was mysteriously begotten by Osiris after his death. This lawsuit forms the subject of one of the most remarkable literary compositions handed down from the ancient world, which is preserved in Papyrus Chester Beatty No. 1,[2] only recently discovered. When the story told by this papyrus begins the case has already been argued before the Heliopolitan Council for eighty years, and the tempers of the gods are growing short. Horus who, in spite of the passing of this length of time, is represented as little more than a child, claims the throne of his father Osiris by the right of

[1] Sethe *Pyramidentexte*, §§ 316–18.
[2] Published by Dr. A. H. Gardiner, *The Chester Beatty Papyri,* No. 1.

a son to succession. Sēth, on the other hand, declares before the Council : *As for me, I am Sēth, the greatest of strength among the Ennead, and I slay the enemy of Rā daily, being in front of the Barque-of-Millions, and none other god is able to do it. I am entitled to the office of Osiris.*[1]

The divine council, however, is depicted in the story as a vacillating body which cannot make up its mind, and always applauds the opinion of the last speaker. Rā-Herakhty-Àtum, the president, openly favours Sēth, and Isis, who pleads on behalf of her son Horus, is yet too sentimental to be unaffected by the claims of blood-relationship with Sēth. The Council first of all summons Ba-neb-tetet, the ram-god of Mendes, to appear before Rā, and to express his opinion. He comes together with Ptah-Tanen, and Rā says to them : *Pronounce judgment upon the two striplings, and stop them from standing thus and wrangling every day.* Ba-neb-tetet replies with a suggestion that the Council write to Neith, goddess of Saïs, and invite her opinion. This they do, and thereupon *Neith, the mighty, the god's mother, sent a letter to the Ennead saying : Give the office of Osiris to his son Horus, and do not do those great acts of wickedness which are not in their place, else I shall be angry, and the heaven shall crash to the ground. And let it be spoken unto the Master of the Universe, the bull which*

[1] Adapted from the translation by Dr. Gardiner, op. cit.

dwelleth in Heliopolis, Double thou Sēth in his possessions, and give unto him Āntā and Astarte thy two daughters, and set thou Horus in the place of his father Osiris.[1]

With this pronouncement the Nine declare themselves in agreement, with the exception of the Sun-god who favours Sēth, and who, enraged at the taunts of the others, departs to his arbour where he sulks for a day, until he is at last coaxed out by the goddess Ḥatḥor. In this vein the strange story proceeds. Isis, whom Sēth has managed to get excluded from the Council, bribes the god Ānty to ferry her over to the island on which the trial is being held, and by a subterfuge forces Sēth to condemn himself out of his own mouth. Horus and Sēth change themselves into two hippopotami and are harpooned in turn by Isis, who nevertheless lets each go free. Horus is next blinded by Sēth, but his sight is restored by Ḥatḥor. At length there follows a trial of strength between the two gods which to us appears extremely repulsive, in which Horus finally vanquishes his opponent. After yet further trials Horus loses patience and demands that the claim should be settled in his favour once for all. But even now the Council shrinks from giving a decision and orders Thōth to write a letter to Osiris, asking him to pronounce judgment. There

[1] This and the following passages from the papyrus are quoted, with kind permission, from Dr. Gardiner's translation, op. cit.

now follows a correspondence which, in many ways, is the most interesting part of the story. Osiris is indignant that Horus has not been declared in the right long before, and replies : *Wherefore shall my son Horus be defrauded, seeing that it is I who make you strong, and it is I who made the barley and the spelt to nourish the gods, and even so the living creatures after the gods, and no god nor any goddess found himself able to do it !*

This letter was brought to Rā-Ḥerakhty as he sat with the Ennead, and exasperated him beyond measure so that he speedily sent a briefer but much ruder letter back to Osiris, which reads : *Suppose thou hadst never come into existence, suppose thou hadst never been born, the barley and the spelt would still exist !* Deeply offended Osiris now sends back a letter which not only causes the Council to settle the dispute finally in favour of Horus, but also provides for us a useful introduction to the study of this god in his most important capacity, that of the ruler of the Other World. In plain words he tells the Ennead that unless they give a just judgment he will send *savage-faced messengers* to fetch them down into his realm of shades, for he is more powerful than they all. The letter reads :

> *Exceeding good is all that thou hast done, thou inventor of the Ennead in very truth, whilst Justice hath been suffered to sink within the nether world. But look thou at the matter thyself also ! As for*

*this land in which I am, it is full of savage-faced
messengers, and they fear not any god nor any
goddess. I will cause them to go forth and they shall
fetch the heart of whosoever doeth wicked deeds,
and they shall be here with me. Moreover, what
signifieth it that I be resting here in the West, whilst
ye are without, all of you? Who is there among
them stronger than I? But behold they have
invented falsehood in very truth. Is it not so that
when Ptah, the great, south of his wall, the lord
of Ānkh-tawy, made the sky, did he not speak
unto the stars which are in it : Ye shall go to rest
in the West every night in the place where king
Osiris is. And after the gods, nobles and plebeians
shall go to rest also in the place where thou art—so
said he not unto me?*

This letter depicts Osiris as a sinister being who
ruled over a dark and dismal region, a cause of terror
to both gods and men. This view of him was that
originally taken by the solar theology, since, among
the ancient spells employed during the Old Kingdom
for the protection of the dead Pharaoh, is one which
is designed to guard the pyramid in which he is
buried against Osiris, if he should come *with an evil
coming*. But in the Osirian theology itself, which
soon attained such widespread popularity that the
solar theologians were forced to adapt themselves
to it, Osiris stood for man's hope of resurrection
after death. For it was believed that, when Isis

collected the dismembered body of her husband, the portions were first carefully embalmed by Anubis and then, by the magical powers of Isis herself and with the help of spells supplied by Thôth, the dead Osiris was brought back to life. To the ancient Egyptian the culmination of the Osiris legend was this resurrection of the god, for, with Osiris' aid, he too hoped to overcome the seeming annihilation of the grave. The statues (Plate 3) and pictures of Osiris represent him as swathed in white funeral wrappings, or in a tight-fitting costume covered with a design imitating bird's feathers, from which his hands project holding the crook and whip—sceptres of kingship—and the *uas* ⌐, a sceptre carried only by gods. His face and hands are often coloured green, for he represents the vegetation of the earth, continually decaying and reviving, and on his head is usually set the *atef*-crown. This crown consists of the tall white cap which was used as the crown of Upper Egypt, with a feather, symbolic of Truth, attached on either side, and sometimes ram's horns added below.

The principal centre of the Osirian cult in dynastic times was the town of Abydos in Upper Egypt. In this *holy district*, it was believed, Isis had discovered the head of the god, and the local fetish, frequently carved upon the monuments, consisted of the reliquary containing it, mounted upon a pole, and decorated with a wig, plumes, and horns. During the Nineteenth Dynasty it would seem that a commission of some kind was sent to examine the ancient necropolis of Abydos, the result of which was that the tomb of a king of the First Dynasty, whose name was misread as *Khent*, was mistaken for that of Osiris himself, who often bears the title *Khenty-âmentyu*, " Chief of the Westerners " (i.e. of the dead). This tomb, in consequence, became at once a place of pilgrimage, and it was gradually buried under a heap of fragments of votive pottery vessels, which procured for it the modern Arabic name of *Umm el-Gaâb*, " Mother-of-pots." For a long time, however, previous to this mistake, and for centuries afterwards, the tradition that Osiris himself (or his head only) had been buried at Abydos rendered it, in the eyes of the Egyptians, of all places in Egypt that in which a man would most desire to be buried. There he would be *in the following* of the *Lord of Eternity*, and would be enabled to partake of the food offerings presented to the god in his temple as well as to enjoy his divine protection. Even if an Egyptian was prevented by circumstances from ordering his actual burial at Abydos, he could achieve the same result by erecting there a cenotaph or a funerary stela inscribed with the necessary prayers and spells, or else a statue which would stand in the temple and receive a portion of the divine offerings. This last-mentioned was probably a privilege conferred only on important people. A fine example of such a statue is that of Khā-em-uas, favourite son of Rameses II and High-priest of Ptaḥ at Memphis, which is now in the British Museum (No. 947). The dedicatory inscription upon it runs : *The King's son Khā-em-uas made it as his monument, his statue of millions of years, to exist in Abydos for ever over the circle of the Lord of Eternity, a glorious place for invocation-offerings, the greatest place of the land of Truth, the holy district where praise is given to the excellent statues, that it* (i.e. the district of Abydos) *may open its road to this excellent spirit, who resteth on the place wherein is the statue of the King's eldest son beloved of him, the* Sem-*priest Khā-em-uas.* It was further supposed that after death a dead person would wish to visit Osiris at Abydos, there to make petition to the god for a place in his kingdom, and for continual sustenance for his spirit. Accordingly, among the many scenes of funerary ceremonies depicted on the walls of an Egyptian tomb, is generally included one showing the dead person, seated in a boat, proceeding to Abydos.

The most impressive monument erected in honour of the god Osiris preserved at Abydos to-day is the beautiful temple of Seti I, the second king of the Nineteenth Dynasty. Besides a number of halls and chapels dedicated to the Osirian triad, the building contains no less than seven main sanctuaries, the central one being occupied by the state-god Åmen-Rā, and the others by Osiris, Isis, Horus, Rā-Ḥerakhty, Ptaḥ, and the deified Seti himself. The coloured reliefs which decorate the walls of this temple are among the finest achievements of the Egyptian sculptor, and charm the visitor by their splendid composition and the delicacy of their execution. In a corridor opening off the second hypostyle hall are to be seen a series of reliefs which give the temple its final significance. They show Seti I and his son, Rameses II, worshipping the names of all their legitimate predecessors upon the throne of Egypt since the reign of Menes, the founder of the First Dynasty (about 3300 B.C.).

Behind the temple of Seti lies what may be considered the most extraordinary building in Egypt, the so-called " Osireion ". It consists of a large subterranean hall, to which a sloping passage leads down from ground-level. This hall, which is built of sandstone with huge granite piers to support the roof, contains an island surrounded by an artificial water-channel, with two flights of steps leading down from it to the water. Beyond the hall is a large chamber shaped like a sarcophagus, the roof of which is sculptured with representations of the sky-goddess Nūt and religious texts. Now the whole conception of the Osireion is the usual one of a " false tomb " or cenotaph, which should stand on the hallowed soil of Abydos, and procure for the dead Seti all the blessings which burial in that sacred spot would obtain, although his body actually rested far away in the Valley of the Tombs of the Kings of Thebes. But for us the most interesting fact about this building is that it was intended to reproduce in stone the cosmos, as it was conceived by Egyptian mythology. The water in the subterranean channel represented the watery mass of Nūn, which had existed before the creation of sky and earth, while the island rising out of it was none other than the legendary mound, the first part of the earth to rise above the primeval waters.[1] On this hill Rā, the creator, had stood, and every morning at sunrise he stood there again, and so this hill became a symbol of resurrection, for the rising of the sun from the realm of darkness typified the victory of life over death. It was not unnatural, therefore, that, under the influence of Osirian mythology, men came to believe that Osiris himself had been buried on this hill, a suitable place for the tomb of the dying and reviving god, and thus pictures often show him enthroned on the top of a double flight of steps, which are intended to represent the primeval mound. On the island, therefore, within the " Osireion ", the body of Pharaoh would lie, enthroned like Rā, the creator, above his universe, and, like Osiris on the hill of resurrection, victorious over death and decay. This majestic

[1] See above, p. 8.

conception finds an interesting parallel in the
funerary papyrus of the lady Ànhay, preserved in
the British Museum (No. 10472), which contains a
coloured vignette apparently representing a building
similar to that of the " Osireion ". The mummy of
Osiris is shown lying upon the top of a double
flight of steps, which is surrounded by an expanse
of blue water from which rise eight columns, the
latter being depicted, according to the rule of
Egyptian drawing, in plan. At the head and foot
of the mummy a ram-headed god stands with hands
uplifted in adoration. The eight columns indicate
that the picture refers to Hermopolis, the Egyptian
name of which was *Khemenu*, " The-city-of-the-
eight-gods," where, according to one tradition, the
primeval hill had first appeared out of the waters
of Nūn.

Besides his patronage of all who became subject
to death, and his power of enabling his worshippers
to survive it, Osiris was closely associated in the
Egyptian mind with the idea of judgment. It is
maintained by a number of scholars that the idea
was originally solar and entirely unconnected with
Osiris, but, whether this was so or not, by the
beginning of the New Kingdom, the period with
which we are chiefly concerned in this book, Osiris
had firmly established himself in Egyptian theology
as judge of the departed. From the Nineteenth
Dynasty onwards most copies of the Book of the Dead

include an elaborate picture of the judgment of
the dead, accompanied by explanatory texts, and
we will therefore proceed to describe it in detail,
following principally the magnificent example con-
tained in the Papyrus of Any in the British Museum
(No. 10470).

The great hall wherein the judgment takes place
is called the *Hall of the Two Truths*, at one end of
which Osiris sits upon his throne within a shrine.
This shrine is intended to represent a rectangular
wooden coffin, with a vaulted lid surmounted by the
falcon-god Seker, but it has been embellished with
uraeus-serpents after the manner of the gilded
baldachin under which a Pharaoh would sit to grant
audience. The ceiling of the shrine is further
decorated with clusters of grapes, made of glazed
composition, and is supported by elaborate floral
columns. Osiris himself is clad in a tight-fitting
dress covered with feather-design, his face and hands
are green, and he wears the *atef*-crown, and a
collar of beads around his neck, and grasps with both
hands the crook-, whip- and *uas*-sceptres. Behind
him, with their arms embracing his shoulders, stand
the goddesses Isis and Nephthys, and before him
rises a lotus bloom upon which stand the four sons
of Horus, Mestá, Ḥapy, Ṭuamutef and Qebeḥsenuf,
the four deities who presided over the entrails of
a dead person after these had been embalmed and
placed in the Canopic jars. Behind them, again,

hangs the animal's hide which is the cult-cymbol of Anubis.

Along the sides of the hall, each on a separate throne, are ranged the great gods of Egypt. In the front sits the Sun-god Rā-Ḥerakhty, *the beautiful god who is in his barque*, and behind him is his other form, Åtum. The remaining deities are Shu, Tefnūt, Geb, Nūt *lady of the sky*, Isis, Nephthys, Horus *the beautiful god*, Ḥathor *lady of the West*, Ḥu and Såa. In the papyrus of Ånhay these gods are not named separately, but two groups of bearded gods appear, named *The Great Nine* and *The Little Nine* respectively. Besides this company of great gods many other divine beings were believed to be present, and these are enumerated in the so-called " Negative Confession " which forms part of Chapter cxxv of the Book of the Dead, and which must be taken into account if the Judgment Scene is to be properly understood. It was thought that there were forty-two gods acting as assessors, one for each of the forty-two nomes or districts into which Egypt was divided, and in their presence the deceased person, if he hoped for an acquittal, had to deny having committed forty-two specified sins. Thus he says :

> *O thou being, broad of stride, who comest forth*
> *   from Heliopolis,*
> * I have done no evil !*
> *O thou embracer of flame, who comest forth from*
> *   Kher-åḥa,*

I have not robbed !
O thou Nose, who comest forth from Hermopolis,
I have not been covetous !

and so on, claiming that in every way he has lived
up to the standard of conduct imposed by men and
gods.

While, however, he is making this declaration of
innocence a more searching test is being carried out
by the gods Anubis and Thōth. A great balance
stands in the centre of the hall, surmounted by the
ape of Thōth, and Anubis, jackal-headed, kneels beside
it, steadying the swinging pointer with one hand
and the right-hand pan with the other. The heart
of the dead Any is placed in one pan, and a feather,
symbol of Maāt or " Truth ", in the other.   The
human heart was regarded by the Egyptians as the
seat of consciousness ; hence, if weighed against
Truth, the accuracy of Any's protestations of
innocence could be tested. As each denial came from
his lips he would be judged by his own heart in the
balance. If it weighed equal with Truth, then all
was well ; but if it sank in the scales, then it was
heavy with sin and the dead man would stand
convicted by the evidence of his own conscience.
On the left Any and his wife watch the dreadful
process, Any reciting with trepidation chapter
xxx B of the Book of the Dead, a spell which was
intended to prevent the heart from betraying him
to his judges. It runs :

O my heart of my mother! O my heart of my mother! O my heart of my transformations! Do not stand up against me as a witness! Do not create opposition to me in the council! Do not cause the pan to sink in the presence of the keeper of the balance! Thou art my double (ka) *which is in my body, the god Khnemu who makes my limbs healthy, etc.*

Five other beings are grouped beside the balance, who are all intimately connected with Any's existence. First there is his soul (*ba*), in the form of a human-headed falcon, which, as we shall see later on, is required to give evidence at the trial. Next to this is the brick upon which Any's mother had sat to give birth to him, which, in the picture, has been given a human (female) head, i.e. is thought of as Meskhent, goddess of birth. Beneath the brick stands a male figure called Shay, " Fate," the destiny to which Any was appointed, and on the left of the pan containing the heart we see the nurse-goddess Renenutet and the goddess Meskhent in human form. On the right of the balance stands the god Thōth, ibis-headed, holding a scribe's reed-pen and palette, with which he records each movement of the balance corresponding to each of the forty-two denials of sin made by Any. Behind Thōth stands a more sinister witness of the judgment, Āmmūt, *the devourer of the dead,* to whom those who have been convicted of a sinful life are thrown. She is a strangely composite creature, and is well described by the text which accompanies her picture in the papyrus of Hunefer (British Museum No. 9901) : *Āmmūt, whose forepart is that of crocodiles, her hindquarters those of a hippopotamus, and her middle that of a lion.*

In spite, however, of all this impressive parade of divine justice it is assumed in every copy of the Book of the Dead that the dead person concerned is acquitted. This was in accordance with the whole aim of these funerary papyri, which was to secure, by magical pictures and texts, a favourable reception for the purchaser in the next world. Hence, in the papyrus of Any, Thōth announces the result of the weighing as follows : *Hear ye these words in very truth. I have judged the heart of Osiris Any, and his soul (ba) stands up as a witness regarding him. His character has been proved righteous upon the great balance, and he has been found without crime. He has not diminished the offering-loaves in the temples. He has not falsely reduced the tax-corn. He has spoken no idle words while he was upon earth.* This favourable verdict is now ratified by the " Great Ennead of gods " seated along the sides of the hall of judgment. They say to Thōth : *That which has come forth from thy mouth is just. Osiris Any has been proved, and he has done no crime or wickedness against us. Āmmūt shall not be suffered to prevail over him, but let there be given to him bread*

*which has been offered in the presence of Osiris, and
a portion of land, that he may dwell in the Field-of-
offerings, like the followers of Horus.*[1]

The dead person has now been tried and found
innocent, and there remains only for him to receive
his reward. Before this happens, however, according
to the papyrus of Ånhay, the deceased is adorned
with feathers, symbolic of righteousness, by the
goddess of Truth herself. Horus, son of Osiris,
falcon-headed and wearing the Double Crown of
Egypt (see Plate 1), now takes Any by the hand and
leads him towards the throne of Osiris, at the same
time addressing the god thus : *I have come unto
thee, Unen-nefer,*[2] *bringing to thee Osiris Any. His
heart is righteous, and has come forth from the balance
without crime against any god or goddess. Thōth has
judged him by the records, and the verdict of the
Nine concerning him is exceeding correct and just.
Let there be given to him bread and beer which has been
offered in the presence of Osiris, that he may exist
like the followers of Horus forever !* To this plea
Any adds his own : *Behold, I am in thy presence,
O lord of the West ! There is no iniquity in my belly.
I have not told a lie knowingly. There is no wickedness
(in me). Grant that I may be like the favoured ones
who are in thy following !* The reply of Osiris is not

---

[1] The " followers of Horus " were the legendary heroes who
fought with that god during his time upon earth (both as the
solar Horus and as Horus, Son of Osiris).

[2] A title of Osiris, apparently meaning " The Good Being ".

given, but we may assume that he admits Any into his kingdom and assigns to him a portion with the blessed dead over whom he rules.

We have spoken of the principal significance which Osiris possessed in the Egyptian mind, as the god who was able to assist mortals to overcome death and decay. So far, however, we have barely touched on the method by which this victory was to be won. It depended upon a complete identification of the dead person with Osiris. Everything which had been done for Osiris, according to the accepted legend, must be done for his worshipper too, if he, like him, was to triumph over the grave. Not only was he given the name of Osiris in the magical texts inscribed upon his funerary papyrus and tomb-equipment (as in the examples quoted above), his body must also undergo the same process of embalming which had been applied to the corpse of Osiris, in order that it might remain incorrupt and ready again to receive the quickening breath of life. In brief, this process consisted of the evisceration of the body, the soaking of the corpse in a solution of natron (a naturally occurring mixture of carbonate and bicarbonate of soda) for a period of many days, thorough desiccation of the body, and finally the swathing of every part of it in linen bandages. The process of embalming, however, was far from being regarded as a preservative treatment only ; the whole operation, from start to finish, was an elaborate religious ritual, superintended by a priest who recited the appropriate spells at every stage. One of the most important items was the placing of amulets on various parts of the body, which would give to it the same protection which Osiris had enjoyed. Each amulet represented some object closely associated with Osiris or one of the other great gods. Thus the *Tet*-amulet was supposed to represent the backbone of Osiris, the *Tât*-amulet, coloured red, stood for the blood of Isis ; the *Ujat* was the eye of Râ, or else the eye of Horus which had been mutilated by Sêth and healed by Thôth ; the large scarab placed over the heart was intended to stimulate the dead heart to beat again, for this beetle was the emblem of Kheprà, creator of all life ; the two fingers of black stone, placed near the embalming incision on the left flank of the corpse, perhaps represented the two fingers of Anubis, which he must have thrust through the incision in order to eviscerate the body of Osiris. Meanwhile the entrails of the dead person, namely his liver, lungs, stomach and intestines, were embalmed separately and placed in four separate jars. These jars were dedicated to four different gods, the sons of Horus, the jar-lids being carved to represent their heads as follows : (1) Mestà (guarding the liver), human-headed ; (2) Ḥapy (guarding the lungs), ape-headed ; (3) Ṭuamutef (guarding the stomach), jackal-headed ; (4) Qebeḥsenuf (guarding the intestines), falcon-headed. These jars, termed by Egyptologists "Canopic jars", were packed in a coffer which is sometimes decorated with the figures of four guardian goddesses, Isis, Nephthys, Neith and Serqet. The completed mummy was next provided with a mask which showed the deceased as in life, and then enclosed in a series of anthropoid coffins, often very richly decorated.

All that could be done by the embalmer's skill to render the body imperishable had now been carried out, and there remained only the magical ceremonies which would give back to this simulacrum of the dead his living powers. This final rite was called *Opening the mouth,* and it was performed on the day of the funeral outside the tomb in which the deceased was to be buried. The mummy was held upright by an embalmer whose head was concealed by the jackal-mask of Anubis, and a priest then touched the face of the dead with a series of magical instruments, at the same time pronouncing powerful spells which would revive the body's living functions. When the rite had been completed the mummy was laid in the burial-chamber prepared for it in *the house of Eternity,* i.e. the tomb.

CHAPTER IV

THE BOOK OF THE DEAD—THE BOOK OF
ĀM ṬUAT—THE BOOK OF GATES

Apart from a few isolated legends, such as that preserved in Papyrus Chester Beatty No. 1, described in the last chapter, the documents which tell us most about the Egyptian gods are the great religious books, the Book of the Dead, the Book of Him who is in the Underworld, and the Book of Gates, Of these the Book of the Dead is the most important, and will be first treated here.

The term " Book of the Dead " was used by the early Egyptologists to cover almost the whole of Egyptian funerary literature, but it is now generally employed as a designation of a particular religious work, which was frequently copied out on papyrus or inscribed upon the walls of tombs from the New Kingdom to the Roman period (about 1580 B.C. to A.D. 300). Two early collections of religious texts contributed to the making of the Book of the Dead, and these have been named by scholars the " Pyramid Texts " and the " Coffin Texts " respectively. The Pyramid Texts are the spells and prayers which are found inscribed on the walls of the burial-chambers in the pyramids of the

Kings of the Fifth and Sixth Dynasties (about 2600 B.C.), i.e. during the latter part of the Old Kingdom. During the Old Kingdom the official religion of the King and his court was solar. When Pharaoh died he flew up to the sky in order to join Rā and rule with him in his celestial kingdom. This view of the after-life is elaborated in the Pyramid Texts. But, as we have already seen, the popularity of Osiris as god of the next world was at this time growing rapidly, and we therefore find that the Pyramid Texts were gradually being adapted to Osirian beliefs, with the introduction of the legend of that god's death and resurrection and the identification of the dead king with him.

After the collapse of the central government at the end of the Sixth Dynasty, the elaborate funerary cult, which had hitherto been the prerogative of the king and nobles alone, was appropriated by the general mass of people, and the rectangular wooden coffins in which Egyptians of the Middle Kingdom (about 2000 B.C.) buried their dead are covered with selections from the old funerary texts. These texts, however, have been arranged in a new recension ; some of the old Pyramid Texts have been discarded and new material has been added, while the part played by Osiris as god of the dead is greatly enlarged. Scholars call this recension the "Coffin Texts", and these are to be considered the direct ancestors of the New Kingdom Book of the Dead.

PLATE I

THE GOD HORUS, SON OF OSIRIS,
wearing the Double Crown of Pharaoh combined with feathers, ram's
horns, etc.   Relief from the temple of Sety I, at Abydos.   Nineteenth
Dynasty

PLATE II

STATUE OF THE GOD ÁMEN,
holding King Tutankhámen between his
knees.   Granite, Eighteenth Dynasty
(Louvre, Paris)

PLATE III

STATUE OF THE GOD OSIRIS
Dark green stone, Twenty-sixth Dynasty
(Cairo Museum, No. 38,358)

THE BOOK OF THE DEAD

Text and vignette of Spell XCIX.   From the Papyrus of Neferrenpet.
Nineteenth Dynasty (Brussels Museum, No. E.5043)

The Book of the Dead, itself, has become well-known to students of ancient Egypt chiefly on account of the magnificent illuminated copies of it on papyrus which are preserved in museums. The best of these papyri were executed during the Eighteenth and Nineteenth Dynasties, and the finest collection of them in the world is housed in the British Museum, where specimens may be seen exhibited in the Third Egyptian Room. The observer cannot fail to be impressed by these documents, which run to a considerable length (78 feet in the case of the papyrus of Any), and are covered with hundreds of columns of beautifully written hieroglyphic text interspersed with vignettes painted in brilliant colours. In the earlier papyri, such as those of Nu (British Museum 10477) and Nebseny (British Museum 9900), greater attention has been paid to the accuracy of the text than to the attractiveness of the vignettes, although these are carefully drawn, but from the end of the Eighteenth Dynasty onwards the vignettes are greatly elaborated, often at the expense of the text, which is either unduly shortened or has been copied out by an inferior scribe. Eventually the standard of copying became so low that the priests of Ámen, who had secured the throne and formed the Twenty-first Dynasty of Kings, made an effort to improve the state of affairs, and arranged that a great part of the work of copying should be performed by priestly scribes of their own order, and that the secular hieratic script of the time should be employed instead of the antique hieroglyphic. The finest known example of these Twenty-first Dynasty manuscripts, the papyrus of Princess Nesy-ta-nebt-Àshru, is preserved in the British Museum and measures nearly 123 feet in length.

The collection of spells forming what we term the Book of the Dead, was called by the Egyptians *The spells for coming forth by day*, and this title indicates the general purpose of the collection. These magical texts were intended to enable the dead person to come out of the darkness of the tomb or of the Other World into the light of the day-sun, and to possess complete freedom of action after death. The title of Spell 17 runs: *Here begin the laudations and glorifications ; coming forth from and entering the Necropolis ; being glorious in the beautiful West ; coming forth by day in every form which he may desire ; playing at draughts and sitting in an arbour ; coming forth as a living soul.* Although, however, such was the general purpose of the Book of the Dead, the spells which it contains are frequently quite unconnected with it and must have originally had an entirely different use. This is the case, for example, with parts of Spell 17, which are mythological in character, and one gathers the impression that the compilers of the Book of the Dead have included any religious text suitable for recitation as a spell regardless of its contents. Moreover, in addition to the positive aim of securing bliss in the after-life, a large number of spells are concerned with the negative one of escaping from the terrible dangers which confronted the Egyptian after death, whether in the form of malevolent gods and demons, or of physical privations such as hunger and thirst. The main divisions into which the Book of the Dead falls are as follows :

(1) HYMNS TO THE GODS

These are addressed to the Sun-god in his various forms and to Osiris, and are to be found in the published texts of the Book of the Dead under the headings of " Introductory Hymns " and " Spell 15 ". A good example, from the papyrus of Nekht (British Museum No. 10471), runs thus :

Adoration of Rā by the royal scribe and military commander Nekht. He saith : Homage to thee, who art brilliant and mighty, Àtum-Ḥerakhty ! When thou hast dawned in the horizon of the sky, there is praise of thee in the mouth of all people. Thou art become beautiful and young as a disc within the hand of thy mother Ḥathor. Dawn thou in every place, thy heart being enlarged forever ! The divinities of the two Lands come to thee bowing down, they give praise at thy shining forth. Thou dawnest in the horizon of the sky, thou brightenest the Two

Lands with malachite. Thou art Rā-Ḥerakhty, the divine youth, the heir of Eternity who begat himself and brought forth himself, King of this land, ruler of the Ṭuat,[1] chief of the districts of the Other World, who came forth from the water, who emerged from Nūn, who reared himself and made splendid his children !

Living god, lord of love ! All folk live when thou shinest, dawning as King of the gods ! Nūt aspergeth thy face, Maāt embraceth thee at every season, thy train rejoiceth for thee, they bow to the ground a thine approach. O lord of the sky, lord of earth king of Truth, lord of Eternity, ruler of everlastingness, sovereign of all the gods, living god who made Eternity, who created the sky and established himself therein ! The Nine are in jubilation a thy shining forth, the earth is in joy at beholding thy beams, the people come forth rejoicing to behold thy beauty every day. Thou sailest the Heavens daily thou betakest thee to thy mother Nūt, thou traverses the Heavens with thy heart enlarged. The lake o Ṭesṭes is at peace, the rebellious serpent is fallen his arms are bound, the knife has severed hi spine.

Rā saileth with a fair breeze. . . . The South an the North tow thee, the West and the East adore thee O primeval one of earth who came into being o himself ! Isis and Nephthys reverence thee, the

---

[1] The underworld.

crown thee in this barque, their arms are behind thee as a protection. The souls of the East follow thee, the souls of the West jubilate to thee, thou rulest all gods, thou receivest enlargement of heart within thy shrine. The criminal serpent has been given to the fire, and thy heart is enlarged forever when thy mother Nūt assigneth thee to thy father Nūn.

(2) Spells for Protection of the Deceased

The dead person greatly feared that evil beings might attempt to deprive him of some vital organ of his body, especially of his heart, the seat of consciousness. Spell 29 accordingly runs :

Spell for preventing a man's heart from being taken away from him in the Other World : Back ! Thou messenger of any god ! Hast thou come to seize this my heart of the living ? Then this my heart of the living shall not be given to thee !

Innumerable serpents and crocodiles also lay in wait for the departed, and strong magic was needed to keep them at bay, such as Spell 33, directed against the serpent Rerek :

Spell for repulsing the serpent Rerek : O Rerek, do not move ! Behold, Geb and Shu stand up against thee ! Thou hast devoured a mouse, which Rā abhors. Thou hast munched the bones of a stinking cat.

(3) SPELLS FOR SECURING PASSAGE

In the course of his travels through the regions of the Other World the dead person often found his way blocked by a closed portal guarded by fierce demons, and the recitation of a spell was necessary in order to gain admission. Examples of texts intended for this purpose are Spell 146 entitled *Spells for entering the closed pylons of the house of Osiris in the Field of Reeds*, and Spell 149 which enabled the reciter to pass through the fourteen districts of the Other World. Section 10 of the latter reads :

O thou district of Qaḥu, which carriest off spirits and gainest the mastery over shadows! Ye who eat what is fresh, who spew out (?) filth upon that which your eyes see. . . . Ye who are in your districts, cast yourselves upon your bellies until I have passed by you! My spirit shall not be carried off, my shadow shall not be mastered! I am a divine falcon ; frankincense is taken out for me, incense is burnt for me, victims are cut up for me. Isis is upon me, Nephthys is behind me, and a way is prepared for me. O Nāu,[1] bull of Nūt! O Neḥebkau![2] I have come unto you, ye gods, that ye may deliver me, and give to me my splendour for eternity!

---

[1] The name of a divine serpent.
[2] See descriptive list of gods, p. 136.

(4) Spells for Securing Benefits

The general intention of attaining to a blissful existence in the after-life is kept in mind throughout the whole Book of the Dead, and is often expressly mentioned in the text. This is the case, for example, with Spell 110, which is designed to enable the deceased to spend his eternity in the " Field of Food-offerings " (*Sekhet-hetep*), and which, in the Papyrus of Any, opens thus :

Beginning of the spells of the Field of Food-offerings, of coming forth by day, of entering and leaving the Necropolis, of frequenting the Field of Reeds, of dwelling at peace in the great city, the mistress of breezes. May I be master there ! May I be a spirit there ! May I plough there ! May I reap there ! May I eat there ! May I drink there, and do (there) all the things that are done upon earth !

The text of Spell 110 is usually accompanied by a large vignette illustrating the Field of Food-offerings, and the papyrus of Any contains a fine example. It depicts this region of the next world as a fertile country divided up, like Egypt, by streams and canals, which in this case are connected with the celestial Nile. In the uppermost section we see the deceased Any adoring three seated gods who have the heads of a hare, a serpent and an ox respectively ; Any paddling a boat laden with offerings of bread, meat and vegetables ; Any adoring two more gods, one of whom is a hawk perched upon a pylon, and the other a human figure in mummy form. In the second section Any is shown reaping the tall golden grain with his sickle, and threshing it by the usual method of causing oxen to tread it out. Further to the right he adores the symbol of inundation (a phœnix on a perch), and kneels before two great stores of winnowed grain. In the third section Any is shown ploughing with a yoke of oxen, and on the right of this scene is a rather naïve description of the celestial river which waters the fields. It runs : *Mouth of the canal (?), a schoenus* [1] *in length, while its breadth cannot be told. There are no fish in it and there are no serpents in it.* In the fourth and last section of the vignette we see two mysterious boats, each containing a flight of steps. One boat has both prow and stern in the form of serpent-heads, and in the accompanying legend is said to belong to Osiris. On the extreme left of the section is a short text describing this marvellous district and the beings who inhabit it : *The place of the spirits, who are seven cubits high. The corn is three cubits high, and the perfect dead reap it.*

Besides this spell, however, there are many others which are intended to obtain specific benefits in the

[1] About two kilometres (?).

hereafter, often of a very material kind, such as abundance of air to breathe, and food and drink for sustenance. Thus Spell 56 reads :

Spell for breathing air and drinking water in the Necropolis. Recitation by N. O Atum, give thou to me the sweet breath which is in thy nose ! I take possession of that throne which is in Hermopolis. I have guarded that egg of the Great Cackler.[1] I flourish and it flourishes ! I live and it lives ! I breathe air and it breathes air !

Again, in order to cross the great lakes in which the land of the hereafter abounded, it was necessary to have a boat. Hence we find a spell (No. 99) entitled *Spell for procuring a boat in the Other World,* part of which is reproduced on Plate 4, where it is accompanied by a vignette showing the dead man, clad in white linen, seated in a boat beneath the bellying sail. This magic boat, however, which has been conjured up by recitation of the spell, will not allow the deceased to make use of it until he has shown knowledge of the unearthly names by which its several parts are called. The text is arranged in the form of question and answer, as follows :

" Tell me my name," saith the mooring-post. " Mistress-of-the-Two-Lands-in-the-shrine " is thy name.

[1] i.e. the Earth-god Geb, in the form of a goose.

> " *Tell me my name,*" *saith the mallet.* " *Leg-of-Apis* " *is thy name.*
>
> " *Tell me my name,*" *saith the steering-gear.* " *Earth-god* " *is thy name.*
>
> " *Tell me my name,*" *saith the mast.* " *He-who-brought - back - the - great -one* [1] *- after-it-had-gone-away* " *is thy name.*
>
> " *Tell me my name,*" *saith the sail.* " *Nūt* " *is thy name.*
>
> " *Tell me my name,*" *say the oars.* " *Fingers-of-Horus-the-Elder* " *are your names.*
>
> " *Tell me my name,*" *saith the baling-pot.* " *Hand - of - Isis - which - stanched - the - blood-from-the-eye-of-Horus* " *is thy name.*

and so on.

Benefits of an even more miraculous kind are also sought, especially the power to assume any form which may appear desirable. A whole series of spells (Nos. 76–88) are devoted to this object, according to which particular transformation the deceased wishes. Spell 76 has the general intention of *the assumption of every form which one may desire to assume*, while the other spells enable the dead person to change himself into a falcon of gold, a divine falcon, a lotus flower, the god Ptaḥ, a phœnix, a heron, a living soul, a swallow, a serpent, the crocodile-god Sebek, and

[1] i.e. the Sun-god's eye. See above, p. 9.

other beings. Spell 77, in the Papyrus of Nu, runs as follows :

Spell for making transformation into a falcon of gold. Recitation by . . . Nu, justified : I have dawned, I have dawned as a great falcon of gold that cometh forth from its egg. I have flown and alighted as a falcon of four cubits, its back and its wings being made of green felspar of Upper Egypt. I have come forth from the cabin of the Mesektet-barque, and my heart is brought to me from the eastern mountain. I have alighted in the Mānjet-barque, and the gods of primeval time are brought to me bowing down and giving praise to me. I have dawned, I have compacted myself as a beautiful falcon of gold with the head of a phœnix, unto which Rā entereth daily to hear its words. I sit down among those gods, the eldest children of Nūt. The Field of Food-offerings is established for me and I eat there, I become a spirit there, I have abundance there unto my heart's desire. The grain-god hath given me my throat, and I have command of the parts of my head.

From the above text it is obvious that the " falcon of gold " is the Sun-god himself, with whom the deceased wishes to become identified.

(5) SPELLS FOR SECURING ACQUITTAL BEFORE THE TRIBUNAL OF OSIRIS

The Judgment Hall of Osiris and what took place there have already been fully described in Chapter III. It will suffice, therefore, here to remark that the intention of emerging successfully from the ordeal of judgment is kept in mind throughout the Book of the Dead, being chiefly expressed by the constant affirmation that the deceased is *true of voice*, i.e. his testimony regarding himself has been proved to be correct. For the advocate who would plead his cause in this trial, on which his eternity depended, the Egyptian turned to Thōth, the wisest of the gods, who had defended Osiris against the charges made by Sēth and caused him to triumph over that arch-enemy. Thue Spell 18 consists of invocations to Thōth, reminding him that he secured the victory for Osiris before each of a series of divine tribunals sitting in the principal towns of Egypt, and urging him to do the same for the dead person. This spell will be considered further under heading No. 6.

The gods who assisted Osiris as judges in the *Hall of the Two Truths* were regarded as sinister and hardly disposed to be merciful. It was therefore necessary to supplement the claims of innocence (made in the so-called Negative Confession described in Chapter III) by a plentiful use of magic, especially by knowledge of the secret names of the judges, which would give the deceased power over them. The nature of these gods and the Egyptian's attitude towards them is well brought out in the Introductory section of Spell 125. The version in the papyrus of Nu runs :

> *Text to be recited on arrival at the Hall of the Two Truths. Separating the Steward of the Chief Treasurer, Nu, justified, from all evil which he has done. Beholding the faces of the gods.*
>
> *Recitation by . . . Nu . . . Homage unto thee, O great god, lord of the Two Truths ! I have come unto thee, my lord, I have been brought (here) that I may behold thy beauty. I know thee, and I know the name of the forty-two gods who are with thee in this Hall of the Two Truths, who live guarding sinners, who feed upon their blood on that day of reckoning characters in the presence of Unen-nefer. Behold, " The-two-daughters,-the-Merty-goddesses,-mistresses-of-the-Two-Truths " is thy name ! Behold me ! I am come before thee, I have brought Truth unto thee, I have expelled wickedness for thee. I have done no wickedness against mankind. I have not made my dependants wretched.* (Here follows a list of denials resembling the Negative Confession, described above on p. 53.) *I am pure ! I am pure ! I am pure ! I am pure ! My purification is the purification of that great phœnix which is in Heracleopolis, for I am that nose of the lord*

of breezes, which giveth life to all people on that day of completing the Eye in Heliopolis, on the last day of the second month of winter. I behold the completing of the Eye in Heliopolis. No evil shall happen to me in this land, in this Hall of the Two Truths, for I know the name of these gods who are in it.

(6) MYTHOLOGICAL TEXTS

These texts, which in large part have no bearing upon the purpose of the Book of the Dead, are employed as magical utterances regardless of their contents. It naturally follows that, for the study of the Egyptian gods, these texts are of the greatest interest, and the most important one in the Book of the Dead is Spell 17, for it constitutes the oldest theological commentary in existence. The nucleus of the spell consists of a collection of ancient texts which already, by the time of the Middle Kingdom (about 2000 B.C.), were considered by the Egyptians so obscure that an explanation was required. The attitude of mind towards theological problems, as revealed by the commentaries of Spell 17, is an interesting subject for study, but there is no room for such a detailed discussion in this book. It must suffice to say that there is little in the way of profundity and a great deal of naïve and indeed childish interpretation. The commentary would seem to have been the work of an intensely formal mind, which was prepared to concoct any number of explanations which would fit the letter of the text, regardless of whether they were artificial or contradictory. Sometimes, however, the comments on a passage really show an accurate grasp of its subject-matter, and this is the case with the opening section, describing the creation of the world by the Sun-god. A passage of the ancient text is first quoted, and the commentary is then introduced by the question : *What does this mean ?* Thus :

> *My speech begins : I am Átum when he was alone in Nūn. I am Rā when he dawned, when he began to rule that which he had made.*
>
> *What does this mean ?*
>
> *This " Rā, when he began to rule that which he had made " means that Rā began to appear as King of that which he had made, when the lifted-up-of-Shu* (i.e. the sky) *had not yet come into being, when he* (i.e. Rā) *was upon the Hill of the Dweller in Hermopolis.*
>
> *I am the great god who came into being of himself.*
>
> *What does this mean ?*
>
> *" The great god who came into being of himself" is the water, it is Nūn the father of the gods. According to another explanation it is Rā.*

Who created his names, the lord of the Nine.

What does this mean?

It is Rā when he created the names of his members; thus came into being these gods who are in his following.

Again, in Section 15, we find an important reference to a story about the Sun-god which has not been preserved in any other form. According to this passage the god at one time mutilated himself:

Ye gods who are in the presence, give me your hands! I am one who changes into you.

What does this mean?

It is the blood which fell from the phallus of Rā when he began to mutilate himself. Then it became the gods who are in the presence of Rā, namely, Ḥu and Sàa, who are in the following of my father Åtum throughout every day.

In this case the explanation of the passage is entirely artificial, and centres around the original and literal meaning of the Egyptian word *baḥ* " presence ", which is actually " phallus ". Plays of this sort upon words are frequently resorted to in Egyptian religious texts, and a melancholy example is to be found in Section 22 of the same spell.

I am that great cat (Egyptian *mau*) *which splits*

the àshed-*tree beside it in Heliopolis, on that night when the enemies of Neb-er-jer were destroyed. What does this mean?*

This tom-cat is Rā himself. He was called " Cat " (màu) when Sàa said concerning him : Is he like (màu) this which he has made? Thus came into being his name of " Cat ".

In many cases the explanations are, even to our own perception, obviously far removed from the actual meaning of the passage, although here it is perhaps necessary to guard against attributing stupidity to the commentator undeservedly. It is probable that he was interpreting his material in a semi-mystical manner, and therefore was not troubled by the externally curious results obtained. Thus Section 9 reads :

I am Min at his coming forth. I have placed my two plumes upon my head.
What does this mean?

As for Min, it is Horus, Champion of his Father. As for his coming forth, it is his birth. As for his two plumes upon his head, it means that Isis and Nephthys went and placed themselves at his head in the form of two kites, and they remained at his head. According to another explanation, it is the two great and mighty uraei upon the forehead of my father Átum. According to another explanation, it is his two eyes, which are missing (?) from his head.

Of almost equal importance with Spell 17 is the spell which usually follows upon it, to which in consequence the number 18 has been given. This text consists of a series of invocations to Thōth, urging him to plead the cause of the deceased before the gods, and to secure victory for him as he secured it for Osiris. Each invocation asks for Thōth's services before a different Council of gods, these councils being situated in the principal cities of Egypt, and is followed by an explanatory gloss. The text is of great interest owing to the number of mythological events, mainly belonging to the Osiris legend, to which it refers, and we give here a translation of portions of the spell according to the papyrus of Nu, together with a short explanation.

SECTION I

O Thōth who justified Osiris against his enemies, justify Osiris N. against his enemies,[1] *before the council wherein is Rā, wherein is Osiris, in the great council which is in Heliopolis, on that night of the evening-meal in Heliopolis; on that night of the battle and of guarding the rebels.*

GLOSS. *As for the great council which is in Heliopolis, it is Átum, it is Shu, it is Tefnūt.*

[1] This invocation is repeated at the beginning of each section.

As for guarding the rebels, it means that the companions of Sêth were destroyed when he was smitten (?) afresh.

SECTION 3

O Thōth, etc., in the great council which is in Letopolis, on that night of the evening-meal in Letopolis.

GLOSS. *As for the great council which is in Letopolis, it is Horus the Eyeless, it is Thōth who is in the great council of Enaref.[1] As for that night of the evening-meal, it is before the morning of the burial of Osiris.*

SECTION 5

O Thōth, etc., in the great council which is on the two banks of Rekhty, on that night which Isis spent awake, making lamentation for her brother Osiris.

GLOSS. *As for the great council which is on the two banks of Rekhty, it is Isis, it is Horus, it is Mestà.*

SECTION 8

O Thōth, etc., in the great council which is at the great hoeing of the land in Busiris, on that night of hoeing the land with blood, and of justifying Osiris against his enemies.

[1] The name of the burial-ground of Heracleopolis, in Middle Egypt.

GLOSS. *As for the great council which is at the great hoeing of the land in Busiris, it means that the companions of Sēth came, having changed their forms into those of sheep and goats ; then they were slaughtered in the presence of these gods, and at length the blood fell from them and they were handed over for reckoning to the dwellers in Busiris.*

SECTION 9

O Thōth, etc., in the great council of Enaref, on that night of concealing " Great-in-forms ".

GLOSS. *As for the great council of Enaref, it is Rā, it is Osiris, it is Shu, it is Babay. As for that night of concealing " Great-in-forms ", it means that the thigh, head, sides and buttocks of Unen nefer* [1] *were buried.*

SECTION 10

O Thōth, etc., in the great council which is in Restau, [2] *on that night which Anubis spent with his hands upon the back-parts of Osiris, and when Horus was justified against his enemies.*

GLOSS. *As for the great council which is in Restau, it is Osiris, it is Horus, it is Isis.*

The general meaning of Sections 1 and 3 is clear, the events referred to being the defeat of Sēth

---

[1] A name of Osiris.
[2] The name of the necropolis of Memphis, but also used to signify the Underworld in general.

and his companions by Horus after the murder of Osiris, and the burial of the latter god. Section 5 describes the oft-mentioned scene in which Isis mourns for her husband's death. Section 8 refers to the slaughter which was made of the supporters of Sēth after their defeat, when the earth at Busiris was watered with their blood. The statement that Sēth and his companions had changed themselves into sheep and goats is interesting, for it reflects the custom of identifying animals which were sacrificed to the gods with the evil Sēth himself. Section 9 takes us back to the burial of Osiris, whose dismembered body had been collected by Isis after searching for it throughout Egypt, and Section 10 shows us Anubis, her faithful assistant, keeping guard over, or perhaps in the act of embalming a vital portion of Osiris' corpse.

Turning from the Book of the Dead we have now to consider two other " books " which played an important part in Egyptian beliefs concerning the world beyond the grave, but which are sharply divided from it, namely, the *Book of Him who is in the Underworld* and the "Book of Gates". Whereas the compilation of the Book of the Dead was, as we have seen, a very loose one, the spells being largely unconnected and chosen in quite an arbitrary manner, the two books just mentioned possess far more unity, and are both concerned with a single subject, the journey of the Sun-god through the

Underworld during the night. It was believed that between the times of sunset and sunrise, when the sun was invisible, the god still continued his travels, but underneath the earth. During this journey he visited the realms of the dead, shedding his light upon them for a brief period, and also contended with various demons who sought to arrest his course and prevent his rising upon the earth once more. Copious selections from these books were inscribed upon the walls of the royal tombs in the Valley of the Kings at Thebes, and are seen by every tourist in Upper Egypt ; hence some account of them here should enable the visitor to these magnificent hypogea, such as those of Seti I and Rameses VI, to appreciate better the wonderful coloured reliefs of gods and demons which adorn their winding corridors in the heart of the rock.

Now although these books dealing with the Underworld make their first appearance for us in the Eighteenth Dynasty, it would seem probable that they are much older, having previously existed only in copies upon papyrus which have now perished. Just as in the case of the Book of the Dead they were first employed for a funerary purpose on behalf of the Pharaoh alone, and, again like the Book of the Dead, were later extended to the common people, for whom extracts were copied on papyrus during the latter part of the New Kingdom. Their popularity, however, at no time seriously rivalled

that of the Book of the Dead, and their contents
represent what was perhaps the most unfruitful
example of Egyptian priestly speculation regarding
the Next World. It was hoped that the employ-
ment of these texts and the numerous pictures which
illustrate them would assist the departed king to
join the barque of the Sun-god in the evening,
and with his supernatural help to overcome the
perils which beset the path of the dead during the
night.

According to the *Book of Him who is in the Underworld*, which is generally referred to by scholars
under its Egyptian name *Àm-Ṭuat*, the underworld
was divided into twelve regions corresponding with
the twelve hours of the night, and the Sun-god
passed through each region at the appropriate hour.
But he himself is very different from the sun of
day. His nature has undergone a change, and he is
no longer the living Rā but Àuf, which means
flesh, that is to say he is a corpse. Further, he is
represented with the head of a ram, which has
perhaps been borrowed from the sacred ram of
Mendes which was regarded as the soul of Osiris,
and the barque in which he travels sometimes takes
the form of a serpent with a head at each end.
He is accompanied by a crew of gods among whom
Ḥu (*Authoritative Utterance*) and Sàa (*Intelligence*)
are prominent, while the god Upuaut (*Opener of
Roads*) stands in the bows. As Àuf approaches

each locality the gods and demons who inhabit it come forth to tow his barque along the infernal river, while he himself addresses the gods and the dead who dwell there, and in turn receives their hymns of praise. To give anything like an intelligible account of the texts and pictures describing this voyage is scarcely possible in the present state of our knowledge, and it may be doubted if it ever will be. We find ourselves confronted with a host of mysterious beings who are not mentioned elsewhere, while lakes of fire, slaughtered victims and innumerable serpents together make up a veritable nightmare. Moreover, it is difficult for us who live at a time so far removed to grasp the exact sense in which all this was intended. We are apt to stigmatize as " contradictory " the apparently confused ideas which run through these books, as through many Egyptian texts, when perhaps it is ourselves who are interpreting them too literally. Thus when we read that the Sun-god passes certain mounds of sand under which various gods are buried, and that these gods include himself under the forms of Átum, Rā and Kheprà, this is probably not to be understood in a stark, literal sense. It must be remembered that a special Egyptian word *seshem* is used to designate the " forms " under which many of the gods exist in the Underworld, a word which may perhaps be translated " apparent form " (German *Erscheinungsform*) or by the Greek *eidolon*, that is to say their whole existence in these realms is a shadowy one, which belongs only to the watches of the night.

As examples of the creatures who were met with on this underground journey those which occur in the Fourth Division, the kingdom of the god Seker, and in the Sixth Division, may be taken. In the uppermost of the three registers into which the picture of the Fourth Division is divided lies a big serpent, generously provided with two heads at one end and a single head at the other. This latter head is grasped by a god who evidently has the creature under control. This serpent is none other than the deity Neḥebkau, who occurs elsewhere in Egyptian religious literature, and who appears to fill a dual role in mythology.[1] He seems to have been at first simply one of the monstrous snakes which threatened the existence of the dead, but afterwards to have been tamed, as it were, and co-opted as a minister of the Sun-god Rā himself. Here, however, he appears in his unregenerate character as a dangerous monster, and the text written above the picture describes him, although, like much of this Underworld literature, it is not (to us) very illuminating. It reads : *He is in this fashion at his abode of the water-flood, the holy road of Restau. He goeth to every place every day, and he*

---

[1] See Shorter, " The God Neḥebkau," in *Journal of Egyptian Archæology*, vol. xxi, pp. 41 ff.

liveth upon the excess of his utterance. (Variant : *upon the breath of his mouth.*) In the lowest register another serpent glides along, this time with three heads, and above it are depicted fourteen separate human heads, each surmounted by a solar disc. These heads represent the gods of the first fourteen days of the month, which are being carried along on the serpent's back.

In the Sixth Division we are confronted by yet another huge serpent, called Ām-akhu, *Devourer-of-spirits*, from whose back four bearded human heads project. These are the heads of the four sons of Horus, Mestā, Ḥapy, Ṭuamutef and Qebeḥsenuf, the guardian-deities of the Canopic jars. The accompanying text describes Ām-akhu as *invisible to this great god. These beings, however, who live in his folds, they hear the voice of this great god every day. What he does in the Underworld is to swallow the shades and devour the spirits of enemies and over-throw them in the Underworld.* This means that as the Sun-god passes on his way the serpent Ām-akhu and the four sons of Horus are invisible to him in the darkness, but that the latter are nevertheless able to hear his voice. Ām-akhu himself is said to occupy his time in destroying the defeated enemies of Rā and Osiris.

Finally, after overcoming all obstacles put in his way, and repulsing all antagonists, of whom the chief is the great serpent-dragon Āapep, the Sun-god reaches the Twelfth Division of the Underworld, from which he rises to shine upon the earth once more. In this scene gods are again depicted dragging the divine barque, and on the extreme right we see the Sun-god transformed into a living being, the scarab-beetle, while next to him is Shu, god of the atmosphere, ready with outstretched arms to lift up the solar disc into the sky. Below, lying against the sandy cliff of the mountain of sunrise, is a mummiform figure which is called "*Form* (seshem) *of Auf*", i.e. the mysterious " apparent form " of death which the Sun-god has borne during his night journey, but which is now discarded when he rises in life at the dawn of a new day.

The second of the two religious works which we are considering, to which scholars have assigned the name "Book of Gates", deals with the same subject as the *Book of Am-Tuat*, namely the journey of the night-sun through the twelve divisions of the Underworld, but concentrates rather upon a description of the gates or portals which give entrance to these divisions, and of the beings who watch over the gates. One of the chief authorities for the text of this book is the alabaster sarcophagus of King Seti I, preserved in the Museum of Sir John Soane in Lincoln's Inn Fields. This beautiful thing, one of the finest Egyptian antiquities in Great Britain, whether considered from its artistic or religious standpoint, is in danger of being overlooked by the visitor to London, and even by the regular frequenter of the better known London Museums. The whole coffin is exquisitely sculptured inside and out with reliefs and hieroglyphic inscriptions, executed in intaglio, which were once filled with a blue vitreous paste. Most striking of all is the representation of Nūt, goddess of the sky, which extends the whole length of the coffin's floor, her slender figure wrapped around with her folded wings, her arms extended to bear aloft into celestial regions the body of the Pharaoh which once rested upon her. This sarcophagus was brought to England by the Italian explorer Belzoni, who discovered the tomb of Seti I, in the Valley of the Tombs of the Kings, in 1815.

As a specimen of the gates described in this book we may take that which stands at the entrance to the Third Division of the Underworld, which is guarded by a serpent called Qaby. On the left of the picture is shown a leaf of the door itself, and on the right the fortified outwork which guards the approach to it. The double walls of this fortification are surmounted by a *cheval-de-frise*, and the outer wall is defended by nine gods who are labelled *The Second Nine*. At the entrance and exit of the corridor running between the walls, which must be traversed in order to reach the door, stand mummied gods, and against the door itself is the serpent Qaby. The corridor and the space before the door are further guarded by *uraeus*-serpents spitting fire. The accompanying text describes what happens when the Sun-god reaches this gate on his nightly journey, and reads : *Arrival of this god at this portal ; entering into this portal. The gods who are in it praise this great god, saying : " Opened is the portal to the Horizon-dweller, unfastened is the door to the Dweller in the Sky ! Hail and welcome, thou traveller who voyagest through the West ! "* Inscribed upon the door is another text, which runs : *He who is in charge of this door opens it to Rā. Saith Sāa to Qaby : " Open thy gate to Rā, unfasten thy door to the Horizon-dweller ! He illumines the twilight, he gives light in the chamber of the West." When this door is shut after this great god has entered, there is lamentation* (?) *among the dwellers in their portal, when they hear this door close.*

The section, however, of the Book of Gates which concerned the departed soul most nearly was the Judgment Hall of Osiris, which was established between the outwork and the door of the Sixth Division. In the illustration of this scene the out-work is guarded by two mummied gods, named *Righteous-of-Heart* and *Secret-of-Heart*. The picture of the Hall itself differs very considerably from the representations of it with which we are familiar in the vignettes of the Book of the Dead. Osiris, wearing the Double Crown of Egypt, sits enthroned upon the top of a flight of steps, the steps which, as we have seen (p. 50), developed out of the ancient idea of the primeval mound. On these steps stand nine gods, who together make up, so the text informs us, the *Nine of Osiris*. The roof of the Hall is surmounted by a *cheval-de-frise*, and from the ceiling four heads of gazelles project. At the top left of the picture Anubis, jackal-headed, is depicted, while in front of Osiris stands the balance with which the dead are tested. The upright of this balance is in the form of a mummied figure, and of the two pans the right-hand one appears to be empty, while the left-hand one contains the bird-hieroglyph of " evil ". This is quite different from the custom followed by the corresponding vignette in the Book of the Dead, according to which the heart is weighed against a feather, the hieroglyph of " Truth ", and it may be that in the Book of Gates we have a variant conception of the weighing according to which the maxium weight of sin permitted is substituted for " Truth ", which amount the heart must not exceed.

As in the Book of Ăm-Ṭuat, the regions of the Underworld depicted in the Book of Gates abound in strange creatures of all kinds, mummified gods, huge serpents and, in the Eighth Division, mysterious beings who live in water and are shown in various attitudes of swimming. To these latter the Sun-god speaks kindly, promising them happiness and abundance of food and drink, but there are other beings who are not so fortunate. These are the *enemies of Osiris*, so often referred to in Egyptian religious texts, whose dreadful fate is also portrayed in the Eighth Division. These " enemies " are shown in a row, their arms bound together in agonizing positions, while a gigantic serpent called Khety belches fire upon them from its mouth. On the left stands Horus, son of Osiris, a bearded figure who leans upon his staff while he informs the captives of their doom. *Ye shall be hacked to pieces,* he says, *and shall not exist ! Your soul shall be destroyed, it shall not live, because of that which ye did to my father Osiris ! . . . O my serpent Khety . . . open thy mouth, unclose thy jaws, belch forth thy fire against the enemies of my father, burn thou up their bodies, consume their souls by this scorching breath of thy mouth, and by the fire that is in thy belly !*

The whole scene is described in the same text as *that which Horus hath done for his father Osiris. These enemies are in this fashion ; Horus ordereth their dooms for them.*

At length the Sun-god reaches the twelfth and last portal of the Underworld, which bears the name *Jesert-bau* " Rich-in-souls ". Passing through this and the door lying behind it, the god enters the region from which he rises to shed his light upon the world at the dawn of a new day. The entire background of this picture is filled with the wavy lines which, according to a convention of Egyptian art, indicate water, and which here represent the primeval watery abyss of Nūn with which the Earth is surrounded. Within these waters we see the god Nūn himself at the bottom of the scene, a large bearded male figure, raising aloft upon his hands the *Mānjet* or morning-barque of the Sun-god. A line of hieroglyphic text explains that *these two arms come forth from the water and bear aloft this god*. In the middle of the barque is the Sun-god in the form of a scarab-beetle, pushing up the solar disc, which in turn is received into the Heavens by the sky-goddess Nūt. The scarab itself is being lifted up by the goddesses Isis and Nephthys, and the rest of the boat's crew consists of Geb, Shu, Ḥeka (" Magic "), Ḥu, Sâa, and three gods who appear to be personifications of doors of some kind. The goddess Nūt, who, as the accompanying text informs us, *receives Rā*, stands upside down upon the head of a curious, elongated male figure, whose body is bent round in a circle so that his toes touch the back of his head. A short text tells us that this is *Osiris who encircles the Underworld* (Ṭuat), and shows that the region of the Ṭuat or Underworld, through which the Sun-god has been passing, is here thought of as an island floating in the waters of Nūn.

CHAPTER V

THE NATURE OF THE GODS—THE GODS AND MAGIC—THE MONOTHEISM OF KING AKHENÁTEN

To modern thinkers, accustomed to the Christian, Jewish and Moslem conceptions of a Supreme Being, the word "god" suggests unlimited power, an entity who is far removed from the weakness of mortals and who holds them completely at his mercy. Such, however, is not the idea of polytheistic peoples in general, and still less was it that of the ancient Egyptians in particular. The fact that the Egyptians divided the inhabitants of the universe into three classes, *men, gods, and the dead*, is sufficient indication that the gods were not looked upon as so very different from either men or the dead. That the gods were regarded as beings greatly superior to men is obvious from the most casual perusal of Egyptian religious texts, but it becomes equally clear that this superiority was not supposed to prevent men from actually obtaining control over them. The medium through which the gods acted was a mysterious power called in Egyptian *heka*, a word which we translate by "magic". It was by means of *heka* that they performed their acts of creation or administration in the universe, and to mortal man, who desired to rise successfully above the limitations of his earthly state, this same *heka* promised power and prosperity. We see this idea, expressed in its most primitive form, in an ancient composition [1] found in the Pyramid Texts of the Fifth Dynasty (about 2600 B.C.), but certainly of predynastic origin (i.e. before 3300 B.C.), a composition which has probably never been surpassed in elemental vigour and unrestrained savagery. It describes how the Pharaoh, Unàs by name, who has just died, arrives in the sky amid the consternation of the elements, and how he thereupon proceeds to hunt down the gods and to cook and eat them like sacrificial cattle, in order to assimilate their magic (*heka*) into himself ! The text reads :

The sky is overclouded, the stars rain down (?), the Bows move about, the bones of the Earth-god tremble, they are still, the Pleiades (?), when they see Unàs appearing as a soul (ba), as a god who lives upon his fathers and feeds upon his mothers ! Unàs is a lord of wisdom whose name his own mother knows not. The glory of Unàs is in the sky, his power is in the horizon, like Àtum his father who fashioned him—yea he fashioned him, but he (Unàs) is more powerful than he !

The doubles (kau) of Unàs are about him, his

---

[1] K. Sethe, *Die Altægyptischen Pyramidentexte*, §§ 393 ff.

*qualities are under his feet, his gods are upon him,
his uraeus-serpents are on his head, the guiding-
snake is on his forehead . . . his powers protect him.
Unàs is the Bull of the sky, with heart keen to thrust,
that lives upon the being of every god, that eats
their entrails, when they come after filling their
bellies with magic (ḥeka) on the Island of
Flame.*

.   .   .   .   .

*Unàs is a lord of food-offerings, who ties the cord,
who prepares his own meal. Unàs eats men and
lives upon gods, lord of carriers, sender of messages.*

*It is Grasper-of-horns . . . who lassoes them for
Unàs. It is the serpent Splendid-of-head which
watches them for him and who drives them to him.
It is the Dweller-upon-the-willows who binds them
for him. It is Wanderer-with-all-knives who
strangles them for Unàs ; he cuts out for him their
entrails, he is the messenger whom he sends to
punish. It is He-of-the-winepress who cuts them
up for Unàs, who cooks for him a portion of them
in his cooking-pots of the evening.*

*Unàs eats their magic and swallows their spirits.
Their great ones are for his morning meal, their
middle-sized ones are for his evening meal, their
little ones are for his meal of the night. Their old
men and their old women are for his incense-
burning. The Great-ones-north-of-the-sky place fire
to the kettles for him, the fuel beneath being the*

thighs of their eldest ones. The dwellers in the sk
serve him, and the cooking-pots are wiped out fo
him with the thighs of their women.

. . . . . .

Unàs has reappeared in the sky, he is crowne
as lord of the horizon. He has smashed the vertebra
and the spinal marrows, he has carried off the hearl
of the gods. He has eaten the Red Crown, he ha
swallowed Uajyt. Unàs feeds upon the lungs of th
wise, he is sated with living on hearts and thei
magic . . . He flourishes, and their magic is in hi
belly, his dignities are not taken from him. He ha
swallowed the understanding of every god.

This brutal poem describes how Unàs, and th
divine beings who assist him, treat the unfortunat
gods in exactly the same way in which we se
cattle for sacrifice being treated in the reliefs upo
the walls of Egyptian temples and tombs. Th
victims are first lassoed and thrown, and their leg
bound together. Then they are slaughtered and cu
up into joints. But the purpose of Unàs in killin
and devouring the gods is made abundantly clea
in the last paragraph. By eating their hearts an
other internal organs he assimilates all their wisdon
and divine power, *their magic is in his belly.* Crud
and indeed revolting as is the form in which thi
idea finds expression here, it stands, nevertheless
at the beginning of that long development of man'
realization that he needed an infusion of divin

power which was to culminate in the spiritual doctrine of the Christian Eucharist.

The Egyptian notion, then, was often not one of dependence upon a god's free gift, but of forcing the god to part with it. Control had to be secured over him, and this was obtained by magical means, such as by learning some word of power against which the god would be helpless, or by finding out his secret name. *I know you, I know your names!* is the cry constantly repeated in religious texts, for there was no surer way of bending a man or a god to one's will than by the correct magical use of the individual's name. This belief is well brought out in the legend of Rā and Isis, which is preserved in two copies, one in a papyrus at Turin and the other in Papyrus Chester Beatty No. XI in the British Museum. According to this story the goddess Isis was originally a woman who was ambitious of becoming mighty among gods and goddesses, and being deeply versed in magic she determined to use this art in order to gain her end. She was aware that the Sun-god Rā possessed a secret name which was of infinite potency, and that, if she could only learn it, she would be able to dominate the whole pantheon by using it as a word of power. Now she observed that Rā had grown old, and that, as happens sometimes with old men, he dribbled at the mouth. Taking, therefore, some of his spittle, she mixed it with earth and kneaded the paste into the form of a magic serpent, which she placed in the path along which the Sun-god would travel in his course across the sky. When Rā reached the spot the serpent bit him, and the god was immediately plunged into agony as the poison flowed through his veins, presumably because, though creator of the universe, he had not created this particular snake, and therefore was vulnerable to its attack. Crying aloud with pain Rā summoned to his side his children the gods, to see if by their power they could cure him. But the gods could only lament, and now Isis was swift to seize the opportunity for which she had been waiting. Approaching the Sun-god she inquired : *What is this, O divine father ? What is it ? Hath a serpent poisoned thee ? Hath something that thou hast fashioned lifted up its head against thee ? Verily I will overthrow it by potent spells ! I will cause it to retreat at the sight of thy splendour !* Then *the holy god opened his mouth*, and described to Isis how he had been suddenly attacked by the serpent in the course of his journey, and how the pain in his body was agonizing. *In sooth it is not fire !* he exclaimed, *It is not water ! For I am colder than water, I am hotter than fire, and all my members sweat. Mine eye trembles so that I cannot see the sky, and water breaks out upon my face as in the time of Summer.* And Isis replied : *Tell me thy name, O divine father, for a man lives when his name is pronounced.*

And Rā replied : *I am he who made the earth, fixing the mountains and creating all that is upon it. I made the water and caused Meht-urt to come into being. . . . I made the sky and concealed the two horizon-gods, and I placed the soul of the gods therein. I am he who opens his eyes and daylight appears, who shuts his eyes and darkness falls, at whose command the waters of the Nile burst forth, whose name the gods know not. I am the creator of hours and the maker of days. I open the festivals of the year and create the river. . . . I am Kheperà in the morning, Rā at noon-day and Àtum in the evening !* But the Sun-god was not cured, for he had not yet mentioned his secret name. So Isis pressed him further, saying : *Thy name hath not been told among the things which thou hast said to me. Declare it to me, and the poison shall come forth, for a man lives when his name is pronounced !* Then at length the stricken god realized that he was in her power, and so, taking her on one side he revealed the awful name, at the same time forbidding that it be divulged to anyone but her son Horus. We are not told what the secret name was, but only that Isis, now become the most powerful of goddesses, cast out the poison from the body of Rā by its magical potency.

With the example of their own gods before them it is not surprising that the Egyptians sought to copy their use of magic in order to obtain the upper hand, and the religious texts frequently show a

conscious superiority over the deity who is being
addressed. An interesting example of this is to be
found in an inscription cut upon the plinth of the
statue of Khāemuas, already mentioned (p. 48),
in the British Museum. Khāemuas was not only a
favourite son of Rameses II and High-priest of the
god Ptaḥ at Memphis, he was also a great magician,
whose fame was preserved in popular stories as late
as the Roman period. In this text, addressed to
Osiris, ruler of that Other World into which
Khāemuas was to pass, we find no humble petition
from a suppliant but an arrogant demand for
recognition, since the glory of the god depends upon
Khāemuas and their two natures are inter-
dependent ! The great High-priest, with an impressive recital of his own ritual and magical
activities, speaks to Osiris as to an equal.
O Osiris, he says, *greatest of the gods, more glorious
than he who made him, mayest thou behold that which
the King's Son and* Sem-*priest Khāemuas doeth ! He
hath caused thee to become great of form, he liveth
through thee, O god, and thou livest through him.
Mayest thou appoint him as thy sole chamberlain !
He is a protector who goeth about the Necropolis, one
who knoweth the road of passing. . . . He openeth the
mouth of Seker himself; he hath created magic in
the womb of Nūt, he openeth the Royal Placenta . . .
he is one who seizeth the arms of thine enemies every
day. Mayest thou appear gloriously in* (or *through ?*)

*im as lord of the nome of Abydos, according as thou
ive unto him life, stability, well-being and duration
1 thy temple, for he is thy son and thy champion.*

So speaks the priest and magician, but his words
o not by any means mark the limit to which the
gyptian sorcerer was prepared to go. He thought
othing of even threatening the gods in order to
btain the fulfilment of his desires. In Spell 65
f the Book of the Dead the deceased is making
he oft-repeated request for justification against
is enemies before the tribunal of gods which judged
he dead. But on this occasion he tells his gods that
: his prayer is not granted he will cause the whole
rder of the universe to be upset, whereas, if it is
ranted, that order shall be maintained. *If thou
ilt not grant me to come forth in triumph over him,*
e says, *in the council of the great god, in presence
f the great Nine, Ḥāpy* (the Nile-god) *shall go up
ɔ the sky and live upon Truth, while Rā shall come
own to the water and live upon fish! But if thou
rant me to come forth against mine enemy and to
riumph in the council of the great god, then Ḥāpy
hall not go up to the sky and live upon Truth, and Rā
hall not come down to the water and live upon fish, but
:ā shall come forth to the sky and live upon Truth,
nd Ḥāpy shall go into the water and live upon fish.*
.gain, in a magical text preserved in the British
Iuseum (Papyrus Chester Beatty No. VIII), the
nagician desires to know the name of a particular

sorcery which is being used against him, knowledge
of which, according to the usual idea, will enable
him to defeat it. He appeals to Osiris to furnish
this information, telling him that this hostile magic
has revealed certain divine secrets, and hoping that
in revenge for this Osiris will be willing to help him
If, however, Osiris refuses to give the necessary
information he threatens the god with appalling
disasters. *He* (i.e. the magic) *has told the secrets of
Osiris and the nature of the gods, and the Nine
are at his call in the Great Place. But if Osiris does no
know his name, I will not permit him* (i.e. Osiris)
*to fare down to Busiris, I will not permit him to sail up
to Abydos, I will tear out his soul and destroy his
corpse, and I will set fire to every tomb of his!*

So far in this chapter we have dwelt only upon
the materialistic conceptions held by the Egyptians
in regard to their gods, let us now turn to consider
the spritual doctrines which can be observed in their
religion. As might be expected it will be found
that their beliefs become the more exalted the more
that they attribute omnipotence to any one
particular deity, in other words the nearer they
approach to a henotheism. It is obvious that if one
god is elevated to a position far above his fellows,
and if theology ascribes to him a supreme rôle both in
the creation of the universe and its inhabitants—
including the other gods—and in the administration
of it, the more likely is man to approach this god

in a spirit of humility and dependence upon divine favour, and the less prone does he become to regard him as merely a superior being who must be cajoled or threatened into compliance with his wishes. We have already mentioned (p. 10) the lofty ideas surrounding the god Ptaḥ which were formulated by the priests of Memphis in their version of the creation of the world, but the deity who at an early period obtained a supremacy which was to provide a foundation for all that was best in the Egyptian religion was the Sun-god Rā-Ātum-Ḥerakhty. During the first great period of Egyptian civilization, the Old Kingdom, when, for the first time, Egypt was being transformed into a fully organized state, the Sun-god was worshipped as chief of the gods, the bodily father of the reigning Pharaoh who laid down the laws and from whom all visible authority proceeded. It was natural, therefore, that there should develop in men's minds a close association between the Sun-god and *Maāt*, the principle of Truth, of Justice, and of the correct ordering of the universe. Rā ruled in the sky as a divine king, the celestial counterpart of Pharaoh, a monarch who governed gods and men alike with absolute justice. He was said to live upon Truth (*Maāt*), and everything which offended against this principle was hateful to him, and in the next world he would require of every man an account of his actions before admitting him to the regions of the sky. Thus the justice of Rā became a strong incentive to the living of a righteous life according to the code of the time, and man was, at any rate in theory, disposed to order his actions with care as he reflected upon *that balance of Rā in which he weighs Truth every day*. The self-laudatory inscriptions carved upon the tomb-walls of the princes and officials of the Old Kingdom, in which they represent their lives as models of perfection, however tiresome they may be to read, at least indicate the existence of this ideal, for the dead men are here setting out their claim for a reward of virtue, that they may be *honoured before the great god*. When, during the Middle Kingdom, the god Osiris finally took the place of the Sun-god as judge of the dead, the principles of Truth and Justice (*Maāt*) on which the solar doctrine had been based were taken over by him, and henceforward it was he who examined the souls of men in the Hall of the Two Truths. But it was still the Sun-god who remained the most *visibly* important of the gods, for Osiris, ruling over the shades, belonged essentially to the realms of the dead in the Other World, and it was out of the solar theology that the most remarkable phase of the Egyptian religion was to develop and linger for a brief space, namely, a conception of monotheism.

When, during the Eighteenth Dynasty, the Theban Pharaohs turned their attention for the first time to foreign conquest upon a large scale, they saw in Ámen, god of Thebes, the giver of their victories. His influence increased steadily both at home and abroad. He had already been identified by his priests with Rā, the most important of the gods, and eventually the High-priest of Ámen at Karnak found himself the director of the priest-hoods of all the Egyptian gods throughout the country. He was in charge also of the rich treasuries and estates of Ámen's temple, and sometimes even occupied civil posts of the highest importance, as when Queen Ḥatshepsut appointed Ḥapusenb to the office of Vizier. Not only was a large portion of State revenue and of the spoils from the yearly campaigns assigned to Ámen, his domains were not confined to Egypt itself, but included three towns in the Lebanon. His fame spread far and wide ; in Canaan he was worshipped as the equal of Baal and Ashtoreth, and his temples arose in the cities of Syria, Palestine, and far south in Nubia at various places, including Napata which was destined to be the god's stronghold in the closing years of Egyptian history. Ámen had become the supreme god of Egypt, and also of the Egyptian empire, which embraced a large part of the then-known world. It is not surprising, therefore, if the mind of the intelligent Egyptian of the time began to turn away from its former narrow conception of a god to a more universal one. Ámen-Rā had become a deity who claimed world-wide allegiance, for he was the beneficent creator and father of all mankind, not of the Egyptians only. He was *Atum, the creator of mankind, who distinguished their nature and made their life ; who made the colours (of men) different, one from another.*[1]

Thus the ground was already prepared for the seed which was soon to blossom into the strangest of all those plants which grew so luxuriously in the jungle of the Egyptian religion. The initiators of the strange movement which we are about to describe were almost certainly the priests of the Sun-god Rā at Heliopolis. For a long time, since the rise of the Eighteenth Dynasty, this priesthood had been jealously regarding the sudden leap to power of Amen, who had before been little more than a local god. The position of this upstart deity, as the Heliopolitan priests must have considered him, was moreover secured by his identification with their own god Rā. Without claiming to be the equivalent of the Sun-god Amen could never have occupied successfully the position of State-god, for the whole nature of the Egyptian kingship, on which the State rested, was solar. The priests of Heliopolis, therefore, seem to have come to the conclusion that they could foster this solar conception of the kingship, namely the belief that Pharaoh was the son and earthly

[1] From the Great Hymn to Amen, preserved on a papyrus at Cairo.

embodiment of Rā, in such a way that Ámen, whose weakness lay in the fact that in reality he was not solar at all, would be excluded. The steps by which the priests of Rā approached their goal can only be detected by us here and there, as when, according to a tablet at Gīzeh, Thothmes IV, while still only a prince, was promised the throne by the Sun-god Harmachis-Kheprà-Átum if he would clear away the sand from his image, the great Sphinx of Gīzeh.

It is during the reign of his son Ámenḥetep III that signs of change are visible, when the use of the word *áten* as a name of the Sun-god first becomes frequent. This word had long been employed to denote the visible disc of the sun from which Rā shone forth upon the world, so that we find expressions such as *Rā and his* áten, and the epithet applied to him : *he who is in his* áten. By the time of Ámenḥetep III, however, a development had taken place, and the *áten* was regarded actually as a form of the Sun-god ; thus to the series of names by which he had been known from primeval times, i.e. Rā, Átum, Horus and Ḥerakhty, was now added a new one " Áten ". During the reign of Ámenḥetep the use of this name became very frequent indeed, and the king seems to have called the palace which he built on the west bank of the Nile at Thebes, " Áten Gleams " ; we know also that he gave this title to the royal barge in which he sailed with his queen Tiy upon the lake attached

to this palace, and even occasionally added the
words to his own name in the cartouche. Thus
there is strong evidence that by now there had
arisen a cult of Åten as a deity distinct by himself,
and we know for certain that a temple of Åten
existed at Thebes in the reign of this king. Con-
ditions, therefore, seem to have been ripe for some
kind of revival of sun-worship, but it is improbable
that this would have occurred in an unorthodox
way if the successor of Åmenhetep, whom he
associated with himself as co-regent about 1380 B.C.,
had not been an unbalanced genius.

The new king was called, like his father, Åmenhetep, but in every other respect he was dissimilar.
The statues and reliefs show him to us as a man of
curious physical appearance, amounting perhaps
to deformity, and his actions prove him to have
possessed the mind and outlook of a fanatic.
Åmenhetep IV, who at once took over the reins
of government from his aged father, was determined
to bring about the final accomplishment of the
return to the old solar cult. The Sun-god was to
gain a complete triumph over Åmen of Thebes, but
in a manner of which the Heliopolitan priests
could never have dreamed, for Åmenhetep IV not
only proclaimed Åten as the chief of the gods, he
proclaimed him as the only god, to the exclusion of
all others. The religion of Egypt, like those of some
other countries, had often produced a *henotheism*,

that is to say, the worship of one deity as supreme among a number of others—the cults of Ámen and Rā were themselves examples of it—but the conception that only one god existed, i.e. *monotheism*, was as entirely new in Egypt as it was elsewhere, except among the Hebrews. But Ámenḥetep IV left no doubt in men's minds regarding what he believed. Not only were the temples of Ámen shut and his priesthood dispossessed, his very name and image was chiselled off the monuments throughout the length and breadth of Egypt, and the word "gods" was likewise obliterated. Moreover the King changed his name from Ámenḥetep, meaning *Ámen-is-content*, to Akhenáten, *It-is-well-with-Áten*, and almost at once began laying plans for moving his place of residence from Thebes, which was full of the associations of the old faith, to some fresh site which he could hallow with his doctrine. This site he found 200 miles north of Thebes, at the modern Tell el-Amarna, where a city began to spring up suddenly at his orders, in which we find both him and his court established by the sixth year of his reign. In this city, which he named Akhetáten, *The-horizon-of-Áten*, he passed the remaining eleven years of his life, surrounded by a fawning court which pretended to drink in his doctrines, spending his time in great religious ceremonies in honour of his god, while the Egyptian empire in Syria-Palestine steadily deteriorated before the Hittite

advance, the revolt of the dynasts and the in-
roads of the Habiru. The religious feelings of the
whole of Egypt must have been bitterly out-
raged by the proscription of the cult of Ámen and
the discouragement of the worship of the other
gods, and it is not surprising that when Akhenáten
died his religion died with him. Smenkhkarā, his
successor, barely survived him, and Tutānkh ten,
who now found himself upon the throne, soon
changed his name to Tutānkhâmen (*Beautiful-is-the-
life-of-Ámen*, instead of *Beautiful-is-the-life-of-Áten*),
and moved his capital back to Thebes. Within a
few years the city of The-horizon-of-Áten became
deserted, and the first and only attempt of Egyptian
theology at monotheism was forgotten.

Though the scope of this book has only allowed
us to treat of the historical events very briefly, it is
fitting that the god whose worship was proclaimed
so suddenly and dramatically by Akhenáten should
be considered in greater detail. The first thing
to be noted is that Akhenáten dispensed with all
anthropomorphic representations of his god, a very
remarkable departure from the traditional Egyptian
usage. The old images of the Sun-god as a man,
or as a man having a falcon's head, he replaced
by an entirely new one, the adequacy and simplicity
of which call for admiration. Henceforward the
supreme god was pictured as he himself actually
appeared, namely as the glowing disc of the sun,

the source of all life. From this disc a multitude of
rays extended downwards, each ray ending in a
human hand which, in the reliefs, is shown caressing
the king and his family who stand beneath. Yet
Áten was certainly not regarded as an impersonal
principle, for he is addressed in the religious texts
as a personal god, hence it would seem that the
solar disc was deliberately chosen to represent him
in order to prevent anthropomorphization, it being
argued, perhaps, that man would do well not to go
further than the god's visible manifestation. This
view is supported by a passage on one of the
boundary-stelae at Amarna, which speaks of Áten
as *he who fashioned himself with his hands, whom no
artificer hath known*. On the other hand, the
traditional notion of an Egyptian god as a king was
heavily emphasized with regard to Áten. Not only
do the texts assert that Áten reigned as king in the
sky while his son Akhenáten reigned upon earth,
but the disc is always shown wearing the royal
uraeus, the god's name is written in cartouches like
that of a Pharaoh, and he is even supposed to cele-
brate festivals of jubilee at the same time as
Akhenáten himself. The cartouches of the Áten
are especially interesting, for they represent a careful
statement of the nature of the god which is un-
paralleled in Egyptian religion, and which
approaches very closely to the definitions of a creed.
There were two editions of these titles, the first

reading : *Lives Rā-Horus-of-the-horizon, rejoicing in the horizon in his name of " Shu-who-is-Àten ".* Later on, however, Akhenàten seems to have felt that the mention of the gods Horus and Shu [1] was objectionable, for the titles were changed to : *Lives Rā, the ruler of the horizon, rejoicing in the horizon in his name of " Rā-the-father-who-has-returned-as-Àten ".*

The tightening up of the solar doctrine indicated by this change is typical of the whole story of Àtenism. At the beginning of his reign Akhenàten professed something not very different from the ortho-dox religion of Heliopolis. Thus his creed mentions Rā-Ḥerakhty (Rā-Horus-of-the-horizon), an ancient form of the Heliopolitan Sun-god, and he declared himself to be the High-priest of Àten, with the title *Ur-maa*, " Great-seer," a title which belonged to the High-priest of Heliopolis. Further, the temples which he erected at Amarna included a building which was called " The House of the *Benben* " the *benben* being a pyramidal stone revered at Heliopolis, and one of the boundary-stelæ, erected in the fourth year of his reign, speaks of provision being made for the worship of the Mnevis-bull at Amarna. These orthodox elements, however, could not restrain his advanced views, and he must have finished by profoundly shocking the Heliopolitan

---

[1] Although, apparently, not Shu, god of the atmosphere, but a word Shu = sunlight.

priesthood, who could never have bargained for the complete overthrow of traditional religion which Akhenåten sought to accomplish. In the city of Akhetåten this strange man adopted the rôle of a teacher, his courtiers and subjects learning *the doctrine*, as it was called, from his own lips. The reliefs of the time show us, over and over again, the king and the royal family worshipping Àten in solemn state in the temple-sanctuary, which, unlike the sanctuary of the ordinary Egyptian temple, was open to the sky, standing before an altar laden with food-offerings for the god, while the many hands of the solar disc extend to his devotees life and benediction. A beautiful hymn addressed to Àten by the king, and in all probability composed by him, is found inscribed upon the walls of certain of the courtiers' tombs at Amarna. It reveals the new faith at its best, describing the loving fatherhood of Àten in moving terms, and begins :

Thou dawnest beautifully in the horizon of the sky, the living Àten, the first to live ! Thou dawnest in the eastern horizon and fillest every land with thy beauty. Thou art lovely, great, glittering high above every land, thy rays encompass the lands unto the extent of all that thou hast made ! Thou art Rā, thou reachest unto their end, and subjectest them to thy beloved son (i.e. Akhenåten). Thou art afar off, yet thy rays are upon earth. . . .

The worshipper passes on to describe how all life depends upon Åten. When he sets in the evening mankind lies down to sleep, but when he shines forth again in the morning sky the earth comes back to life and men rise up to work, *they wash their bodies, they take their clothing, their hands praise thy rising, and throughout the land they do their tasks.* Even the animals and plants thrive happily in the radiance of Åten :

> *All cattle are content with their herbage, the trees and herbs are green, the birds fly from their nests, their wings praise thy double* (ka) *! All wild beasts dance upon their feet, all flying and fluttering things come to life when thou hast dawned for them !*

Åten is the source of all life, and it is he who creates the child in his mother's womb, sustaining him with nourishment until the day of his birth. Then, in contrast, to show how even the most insignificant creature is likewise the product of Åten's loving care, the poet tells of the chick within its egg, how the Sun-god wakes it to life with his quickening power so that it breaks the shell, and comes out *to chirp with all his might. He goeth upon his feet after he has come forth from it.*

In this fatherly manner the Sun-god cares for his creatures, but his activity is not confined to Egypt. In a passage remarkable for its universal outlook we read :

How manifold are thy works that are hidden from me, sole god, beside whom there is none other! Thou hast fashioned the earth at thy desire when thou wast alone, even all mankind, cattle and all wild beasts, and all creatures that are upon earth, that walk upon their feet or go on high flying with their wings.

The foreign countries of Syria and Kush,[1] and the land of Egypt—thou settest every man in his place and suppliest their needs, each man possessing his food, and reckoned is his lifetime. Their tongues are divided in speech and their form likewise; their skins also are distinguished, for thou dost distinguish the foreign peoples.

Thou makest the Nile in the Underworld, and bringest it forth at thy pleasure to give life to the people, even as thou hast made them. . . . As to all distant nations, thou makest that whereon they live. Thou hast set a Nile [2] in the sky, so that it may descend for them and make waves upon the mountains like the Great Green,[3] to wet their fields in their districts. How excellently made are thy designs, thou Lord of Eternity! A Nile in the sky . . . for foreign peoples and all animals of the desert that go on foot, and the (real) Nile, it cometh forth from the Underworld for Egypt!

[1] Nubia.
[2] A poetical description of rain.
[3] The Mediterranean Sea.

The hymn concludes :

> . . . *Thou art in my heart, there is none other that knoweth thee save thy son* Nefer-kheperu-Rā-uā-en-Rā, *whom thou hast caused to be wise in thy designs and in thy strength ! The earth came into being by thy hand even as thou hast created them. When thou hast dawned they live, and when thou settest they die. Thou thyself art length of days and one liveth in thee. Eyes are fixed upon thy beauty until thou settest ; then all labours are set aside when thou settest on the right* (i.e. in the west). . . . *Thou raisest them* [1] *up for thy son, who came forth from thy body, the King of Upper and Lower Egypt who liveth on Truth, Lord of the Two Lands,* Nefer-kheperu-Rā-uā-en-Rā, *son of Rā, who liveth on Truth, lord of diadems,* Akhenâten *of long life, and for the Great Royal Wife beloved of him, Lady of the Two Lands,* Nefer-neferu-Åten-Nefert-ity, *who liveth and is young for ever and ever.*

That this composition is rich in ideas of a high order is obvious at first sight and cannot be denied, but, unfortunately, it has led some modern writers to conclude that these ideas are due to Akhenâten himself, who has consequently been regarded as unique among ancient Egyptian theologians in conceiving them. The contrary, however, is the truth. There is scarcely an idea expressed in the religious

[1] i.e. mankind.

literature of his reign which cannot be paralleled in the sacred writings of orthodox Egyptian belief. In particular, the hymn to Áten itself closely resembles the great hymn to Ámen, preserved at Cairo, which dates back to about the time of Ámenḥetep II, several reigns before Akhenáten. Both these compositions bear a strong likeness to the CIVth Psalm,[1] and the correspondence in certain passages between Akhenáten's hymn and the earlier one to Ámen is so striking that it is impossible not to conclude that Akhenáten has adapted them. In so far as the Áten religion emphasized the fatherhood of the god and his solicitude for all mankind besides the Egyptians, it was simply continuing and developing that universal view of deity which, as we have seen, had already grown up around the person of Ámen-Rā during the earlier part of the Eighteenth Dynasty, as a direct result of the spread of Egyptian empire. The unique contribution of Akhenáten to the history of religion was not this but the doctrine of monotheism, which, as we have already pointed out, is not to be found at this period elsewhere in the ancient world except among the Hebrews. The adoption of this belief by Akhenáten consequently presents one of the most difficult problems in Egyptology. How did it come about ? The step from henotheism to monotheism is a great one, and there is no indication whatsoever

[1] Psalm CIII in the Vulgate.

that the theology of the ancient Egyptians ever
hinted at such a step either before or after the time
of this revolutionary. The other almost equally
curious facts about his religion were the development of the idea of the solar disc with its rays ending
in human hands, and the accompanying refusal to
depict the god in a human or animal form. Although
the starting-point of this official return to sun-
worship was undoubtedly the theology of the priests
of Heliopolis, the latter was soon left far behind.
Áten may have borne an old name but he was
essentially a new god, and consequently an attempt
has been made to find a foreign inspiration for his
existence. The fact that Thothmes IV married a
princess of Mitanni, a country north of the
Euphrates, and that their son Ámenḥetep III and
grandson Akhenáten drew wives from the same
foreign source, has led some scholars to postulate a
Mitannian influence upon the Egyptian religion at
this time.[1] It is known, from the text of a treaty
found at Boghaz Keui, the capital of the Hittite
empire, that the Mitannians worshipped gods called
Mitrashshiel, Uruwanashshiel, Intar, Nashat-
tiyanna, who seem almost certainly to be identical
with the Indian gods Mītra (Mithras), Varuna,
Indra and Nasatiya. The celestial and solar
character of these gods, it is suggested, may have

[1] See Budge, *Tutankhâmen, Ámenism, Átenism and Egyptian
Monotheism*, pp. 21, 113.

encouraged Thothmes IV and Ámenḥetep III to favour a revival of devotion to the old Sun-god of Heliopolis, and have prompted the unexpected developments which took place under Akhenáten. Thus the Heliopolitan Sun-god, in his form of Ḥerakhty, i.e. "Horus-of-the-horizon", may be said to correspond to the Indian Sūrya, the rising and setting sun, and Rā may be equated with Savitri, the sun shining in full strength, who possessed long arms of gold like Áten.[1] The insistence, in the literature of the Áten faith, upon the beauty and power of sun-light makes this suggestion of Aryan influence attractive. But even if this influence existed—and there is not a single piece of tangible evidence that it did—it would not account for the sudden appearance of the monotheistic doctrine. The problem remains unsolved, and we must content ourselves by concluding that the answer lies in the personality of Akhenáten himself, to whose individual and remarkable mind the surprising developments of Átenism are probably to be attributed. It is by no means impossible that he actually was an advanced thinker, indeed the only one whom, to our knowledge, the Egyptian religion produced.

If the monotheistic doctrine of the Áten religion was a great advance upon orthodox Egyptian beliefs the same cannot be said of other teachings

[1] See Budge, op. cit.

of the new faith. The divinity of Pharaoh was more heavily emphasized than ever, and the religious texts constantly speak of Akhenáten as an earthly counterpart of the Áten in Heaven. In the tomb-inscriptions the king is addressed as *maker of fate, creator of good fortune, lord of burial and giver of old age* ; he is *the fate who giveth life,* and *the great Nile of the whole land through beholding whom they live* ; he is *millions of Niles pouring forth water daily . . . my god who made me, by whose double* (ka) *I live !* as well as Rā himself. Thus, as has been pointed out earlier in this chapter, the cult of Átenism was closely bound up with the solar basis of the Egyptian kingship. But whereas in this Átenism might have been regarded as a logical development of orthodox belief, there was one thing in which it was found sadly wanting. In regard to life after death the new religion seems to have been almost silent. The tomb-inscriptions hold out no hope of an eternal existence hereafter in some blessed realm, such as the kingdom of Rā or that of Osiris. They seem to suggest only a vague sort of survival, a ghost-like existence in the tomb. That is to say, only the barest elements of the old orthodox funerary belief were retained, and nothing new was added to make up the deficiency. During this existence in the tomb Panehsy, chief servitor of the Áten, prays to Akhenáten that he may grant him to *behold the living Áten when he dawns, and to adore him,* and that he will allow him *to receive bread that has been offered in the Presence at every festival of the living Àten in the House of the Benben*; likewise he prays to Nefertity for *an entrance in favour and a going forth in love, and a good remembrance in the presence of the King* and among his court. Again he prays to Akhenàten that *he may grant a long lifetime* (or *duration ?*) *of beholding thy beauty, without ceasing to behold thee every day.* Thus it would seem that the dead man hoped to spend his eternity in the following of his king as in life, but there is no indication as to where this was to be, whether in the tomb or in some region of the sky. All is left vague, and, compared with the definite promises made by the orthodox systems of Rā and Osiris, as we find them combined in the Book of the Dead, Àtenism could have held no attraction for the masses. The new religion remained the hobby of Akhenàten and of a compliant court, and with his death it vanished as a dream. No better epitaph for Àtenism could be found than the king's own words, with which he addresses his god in the famous hymn : *Thou art in my heart, there is none other that knoweth thee save thy son Akhenàten, whom thou hast caused to be wise in thy designs and in thy strength !*

DESCRIPTIVE LIST OF THE PRINCIPAL EGYPTIAN GODS

Under the name of each deity are entered, according to his or her importance, all or some of the following items of information :—

(1) The common forms, (*a*) human and (*b*) animal, in which the god or goddess is represented on the monuments.

(2) The principal cult-centre during the Dynastic Period.

(3) The nature of the deity.

(4) A reference to the pages of this book, if any, on which the deity is mentioned.

ÁÁḤ, god.

Bearded man wearing disc and crescent of moon ☉ upon his head : sometimes, however, indistinguishable in appearance from KHENSU (q.v.). A moon-god.

ĀAPEP (Apophis), demon.

A huge serpent, representing storm and darkness, which attempts to obstruct the Sun-god on his voyage. p. 88.

ÁḤY (also called Ḥeru-sma-tauy), god.

Boy wearing the Double Crown ⚚ of Pharaoh

and sidelock of youth ; he often carries a *sistrum* 🎐. Son of Ḥatḥor of Dendera and Horus of Edfu.

ÁMEN, ÁMEN-RĀ (Amon, Amūn), god.

(a) Bearded man wearing a cap surmounted by two tall plumes (see Plate 2). (b) A ram. Cult-centre : Thebes (Luxor and Karnak). Perhaps originally a god of air and wind ; later certainly of physical reproduction. National god of Egypt in the Eighteenth Dynasty and onwards. pp. 13 ff. and *passim*.

ÁMENḤETEP (Amenhotep, Amenophis), son of Ḥapu, god.

Man, sometimes bearded, holding a roll of papyrus. Cult-centre : Thebes. Actually the architect of King Ámenḥetep III, of the Eighteenth Dynasty. Reputed to have possessed great wisdom and therefore later deified.

ÁMENḤETEP I (Amenhotep, Amenophis), god.

An Egyptian King, bearded, sometimes with flesh coloured black. Cult-centre : Thebes. The second king of the Eighteenth Dynasty, deified, and worshipped, together with his mother Nefertáry, as guardian deity of the Theban Necropolis.

ĀMMŪT, female demon.

A combination of crocodile, lioness and hippopotamus. She was present at the Judgment after death and devoured the souls of the condemned. pp. 55–6.

ȦNḤERT (Onouris), god.

Bearded man with one hand (or both hands) upraised, holding a spear ; on his head are four tall plumes 𝄞. A sky god, often identified with Shu.

ȦNQET (Anukis), goddess.

A woman wearing a head-dress consisting of a number of feathers. Cult-centre : the First Cataract (Assuān), where she was associated with Khnemu and Satet.

ĀNTȦ (Anat), goddess.

A woman with the same head-dress as Astarte (q.v.), brandishing weapons. An Asiatic deity of warfare in Egyptian form. Regarded as a daughter of Rā. p. 43.

ANUBIS (Ȧnpu), god.

(a) Man with the head of a jackal (or dog ?) ; (b) a couchant jackal (or dog ?). Cult-centre : Cynopolis (el-Ḳēs). Patron of embalming and guardian of the tomb. pp. 53, 54, 59, 60, 82, 83, 92.

ȦPET, goddess.

(a) Woman ; (b) identical in appearance with TAŪRT (q.v.) ; wears the solar disc and cow's horns of Ḥathor upon her head. Cult-centre : Thebes.

APIS (Ḥap), god.

Sacred bull, with the solar disc and *uraeus-*

serpent between its horns.   Kept at Memphis.
Regarded as incarnation of Ptaḥ and of Osiris.
See also SERAPIS.   p. 72.

APOPHIS.   See under ĀAPEP.

ÀSÀR, ÀUSÀR.   See under OSIRIS.

AST, goddess.   See ISIS.

ASTARTE (Ashtoreth), goddess.

Woman wearing the *atef*-crown (see p. 46),
on horseback, brandishing weapons. Asiatic deity
in Egyptian form, but only as a goddess of war.
Regarded as a daughter of Rā, or of Ptaḥ. pp. 43,107.

ÀTEN (Aton), god.

Name of the disc of the sun. During the reign
of Akhenàten, the heretic king (about 1380–
1362 B.C.), worshipped as sole god and represented
as a disc from which project many rays ending
in human hands.   pp. 109–123.

ÀTŪM (Tem, Tum), god.

Bearded man wearing the Double Crown
of Pharaoh.   Cult-centre : Heliopolis. A form of
the Sun-god, especially at evening.   pp. 4, 7, 30,
42, 53, 65, 71, 77–80, 86, 96, 101, 105, 108, 109.

ÀUF, god.

Man with the head of a ram, wearing the solar
disc between his horns. The form taken by the
Sun-god at night for his voyage through the
Underworld.   pp. 85, 89.

ÅUSĀAS, goddess.

Woman, wearing solar disc and horns of Ḥatḥor. Cult-centre : Heliopolis. Consort of Ḥerakhty.

BACCHIS. See under BUCHIS.

BA-NEB-ṬEṬET (Banebdedet), god.

Sacred ram (or goat ?), with solar disc and *uraeus*-serpent between its horns. Cult-centre : Mendes. Regarded as incarnation of Osiris and of Rā. pp. 42, 85.

BASTET (Bast), goddess.

(*a*) Woman with cat's head, holding a *sistrum* ; (*b*) a cat. Cult-centre : Bubastis. Represents the beneficent powers of the sun ; frequently merged with Sekhmet, and often identified with Mūt.

BES, god.

Bearded dwarf, with shaggy hair and a tail, often wearing a lion's skin. Patron of music, jollity, childbirth ; popular domestic deity. p. 34.

BUCHIS (Bacchis), god.

Sacred bull, with the solar disc and two plumes between his horns. Kept at Hermonthis (Armant). Regarded as incarnation of Rā and Osiris.

BUTO, goddess. See under UAJYT.

DEDUN. See under ṬEṬUN.

DUAMUTEF. See under ṬUAMUTEF.

ERNUTET. See under RENENŪTET.

GEB (Keb), god.

    (*a*) Bearded man with a goose upon his head
(*b*) a goose. The earth-god, husband of Nū
pp. 7, 24, 25, 41, 53, 67, 71, 94.

ḤAP. See under APIS.

ḤAPY, god.

    Mummiform figure with the head of a cyno
cephalus ape. One of the four sons of Horus
Protected the lungs of the dead, which wer
embalmed in the second Canopic jar. pp. 52, 59, 88

ḤĀPY, god.

    Bearded man with female breasts and pendulou
stomach, wearing aquatic plants or upo
his head, and holding a tray of food-produce
or pouring water from vases. God of the Nile
p. 103.

HARMACHIS (Ḥeru-em-akhet), god.

    The name, *Horus-in-the-horizon*, which wa
given to the great Sphinx at Gīzeh. p. 109.

HARPOCRATES, god. See HORUS 2 (*b*).

ḤATḤOR, goddess.

    (*a*) Woman wearing on her head the solar disc
between cow's horns; (*b*) a cow wearing the
solar disc and two plumes between her horns.
A sky-goddess, with many other associations.

Identified with Isis. Nurse of Horus and of the Pharaoh. Patroness of love, and of the necropolis. pp. 9, 53, 65, 66.

ḤEQET, goddess.

Woman with the head of a frog. Consort of Khnemu. Associated with creation and birth.

ḤERAKHTY (Harakhte, Horakhte), god.   See HORUS I (*a*).

ḤERU-SMA-TAUY (Harsomtus), god. See under AḤY.

ḤERYSHEF (Harsaphes), god.

Man with the head of a ram.   Cult-centre : Heracleopolis (Ahnāsya).

HORUS, god.

1. The solar Horus. pp. 5, 20, 57, 109. Represented as a falcon, or as a falcon-headed man indistinguishable from Rā, sometimes wearing the solar disc and *uraeus* Ω. His most important forms are :

(*a*) ḤERAKHTY, whose name means *Horus-of-the-horizon*. Often identified with Rā, when he becomes Rā-Ḥerakhty. Cult-centre : Heliopolis. A form of the sun when rising and setting. pp. 5, 21, 42, 49, 53, 65, 105, 109, 114.

(*b*) HORUS of BEḤṬET. Also represented as a solar disc provided with falcon's wings, which is frequently carved over the doors of temples. Cult-centre : Edfu (*Beḥṭet*).

(c) HORUS THE ELDER (Haroëris).   Cult-centre : Letopolis.   p. 72.

2. Horus, son of Osiris. pp. 21, 25, 38–44, 49, 52, 53, 59, 72, 79, 81–83, 88, 93, 101.

(a) Man with falcon's head, wearing the Double Crown ⍟ of Pharaoh (Plate 1).   Avenger of Osiris and prototype of the dutiful son. p. 57.

(b) ḤERU-PA-KHRET (Harpocrates), whose name means *Horus-the-child*. Infant boy wearing the Double Crown ⍟ of Pharaoh, or the head-dress ⍟⍟⍟, and side-lock of youth, and sucking his finger. The son of Osiris as a child, often shown being suckled by Isis or Ḥatḥor.   Also identified with the Sun-god who, new-born every morning, is shown emerging from a lotus upon the celestial waters. p. 41.

ḤU, god.

Bearded man. His name means *Authoritative-utterance*. Attends Rā in the solar-barque. pp. 53, 78, 85, 94.

IMḤETEP (Imhotep), god.

A priest with shaven head, seated, holding an open papyrus-roll upon his knees. Cult-centre : Memphis.   Actually the adviser of King Jeser (Zoser) of the Third Dynasty, reputed to have possessed great wisdom, and therefore later deified.   Patron of learning, especially medical science, and therefore identified by the Greeks with Asclepius.

IMSETI. See under MESTÁ.

ISIS (AST), goddess.

Woman wearing upon her head ⌡, the hieroglyph of her name. Often represented in statuettes as suckling the infant Horus, who sits upon her lap. Sometimes identified with Ḥatḥor, when she wears the solar disc and cow's horns of that goddess. Sister and consort of Osiris. Proto-type of motherhood and of the faithful wife. pp. 7, 21, 30, 35, 37 ff., 42, 49, 52, 53, 59, 60, 66, 68, 72, 79, 81–83, 94, 99–101.

KEB. See under GEB.

KHENSU (Khonsu, Khons), god.

Young prince, wearing side-lock of youth, and lunar disc and crescent ○ upon his head ; or else a falcon-headed man with the same head-dress. Cult-centre : Thebes. A god of the moon. Son of Ámen and Mūt. pp. 17, 18, 21, 26, 31.

KHEPRÁ (Kheperá, Khepri), god.

(a) Man with a scarab-beetle 𓆣 instead of a human head ; (b) a scarab-beetle. Cult-centre : Heliopolis. A form of the Sun-god in the morning, as the *self-created*. pp. 5, 7, 59, 86, 101, 109.

KHNEMU (Khnum), god.

Man with the head of a ram. Cult-centre : the First Cataract (Assuān). Fashions the bodies of mankind and gods upon his potter's wheel. Consort of Ḥeqet. pp. 8, 55.

MAAḤES, god.

(*a*) Man with the head of a lion, wearing *atef*-crown (see p. 46) ; (*b*) a lion. Son of Rā and Bastet. Often identified with Shu and Nefertem.

MAĀT, goddess.

Woman wearing a feather $\int$ upon her head. Personification of Truth and Justice. pp. 54, 57, 66, 92, 105, 106.

MEḤEN, demon.

Serpent which protects the Sun-god when voyaging in his barque.

MEḤTURT, goddess.

A cow with the solar disc between its horns. Goddess of the sky, when this is regarded as a colossal cow. Often identified with Ḥathor, pp. 8, 101.

MENTHU (Mentu, Month), god.

Man with falcon's head surmounted by solar disc, *uraeus*-serpent and two tall plumes (i.e. Ω combined with $\lVert$). Cult-centre : Hermonthis (Armant). Patron of war. p. 16.

MERTSEGER, goddess.

A large *uraeus*-serpent with a woman's head. Cult-centre : Thebes. Patron of the Theban necropolis. p. 35.

MESKHENT, goddess.

Woman, wearing 𓋏 upon her head ; or represented as a brick with a woman's head attached. Patroness of birth, and identified with the brick on which the mother sat when in labour. p. 55.

MESTÀ (Imseti), god.

Bearded man, mummiform.   One of the four sons of Horus.   Protected the liver of the dead, which was embalmed in the first Canopic jar. pp. 52, 59, 81, 88.

MIN (Menu), god.

Bearded man, ithyphallic, wearing the same head-dress as Àmen (see Plate 2) ;   his right hand is raised, holding a whip. Cult-centres : Panopolis (Akhmîm) and Coptos (Ḳuft).   God of sexual reproduction.   Regarded as another form of Àmen. pp. 14, 79.

MNEVIS, god.

Sacred bull, with the solar disc and *uraeus*-serpent between its horns.   Kept at Heliopolis. Incarnation of Rā. p. 114.

MŪT, goddess.

(*a*) Woman, wearing the Double Crown 𓋑 of Pharaoh ; (*b*) a vulture. Cult-centre : Thebes. Consort of Àmen. pp. 16–18, 21, 26, 31.

NEFERTEM, god.

Bearded man, upon his head a lotus flower from which rise two tall plumes ⬙. Son of Ptaḥ and Sekhmet. p. 11.

NEḤEBKAU, god.

A serpent with human legs and arms. In a bad capacity he was a dangerous serpent of the Underworld. In a benevolent rôle he was a servitor of Rā, and also provided food for the departed. pp. 68, 87.

NEITH, goddess.

Woman wearing the Red Crown ⬙ of Lower Egypt, and grasping a bow and arrows. Cult-centre : Saïs. Assists Isis, Nephthys and Serqet to guard the Canopic jars. pp. 42, 60.

NEKHEBET, goddess.

(a) Woman, or (b) a vulture, wearing the White Crown ⬙ of Upper Egypt. Cult-centre : Eileithyiaspolis (el-Kāb). Guardian deity of Upper Egypt.

NEPHTHYS, goddess.

Woman wearing upon her head ⬙, the hieroglyph of her name. Consort of Sēth. Assists Isis in attendance upon her brother Osiris. pp. 7, 39, 52, 53, 60, 66, 68, 79, 94.

NŪN, god.

Bearded man. Personification of the primeval

watery mass surrounding the world, from which, at the Creation, all life sprang. pp. 6–8, 41, 50, 51, 66, 67, 77, 94.

NŪT, goddess.

Woman with wings outspread or folded around her body, wearing upon her head ☉, the hieroglyph of her name ; or a woman, with elongated body, stooping so that her hands touch the ground. Goddess of the sky, consort of Geb. pp. 7, 30, 40, 49, 53, 66-68, 72, 73, 90, 94, 102.

ONOURIS. See under ÀNḤERT.

OSIRIS (Àsàr, Àusàr), god.

Bearded man, mummiform, wearing *atef*-crown (see Plate 3) : his hands project from his wrappings, holding the crook ⌐ and whip ⋀ sceptres. His flesh is often coloured green or black. Cult-centres : Busiris and, later, Abydos. Judge and ruler of the dead ; supreme god of the funerary cult. pp. 7, 13, 21, 31, 37–60, 62, 70, 74, 75, 80–83, 85, 88, 91–94, 102, 104, 106, 122, 123.

PAKHET (Pasht), goddess.

Woman with the head of a lioness. Cult-centre : Beniḥasan (rock-temple called Speos Artemidos).

PTAḤ, god.

Bearded man depicted in the form of a primitive idol, with legs not separated. His head is shaven and he holds the same sceptre as that held by Khensu (see p. 18). Cult-centre : Memphis. Divine artificer, and therefore identified by the

Greeks with Hephaestus, by the Romans with Vulcan. Patron of arts and crafts. pp. 8, 10, 11, 21, 31, 42, 49, 72, 102, 105.

PTAḤ-SEKER-OSIRIS (Ptaḥ-Seker-Åsàr), god.
Bandy-legged dwarf, clean-shaven, sometimes with a scarab-beetle upon his head. Or a bearded mummiform figure wearing two feathers, solar disc and ram's horns ⚌ upon his head. A funerary god compounded of Ptaḥ, Seker and Osiris.

QEBEḤSENUF, god.
Mummiform figure with the head of a falcon. One of the four sons of Horus. Protected the intestines of the dead, which were embalmed in the fourth Canopic jar. pp. 52, 59, 88.

QEṬESH, goddess.
Naked woman holding flowers, standing on the back of a lion. An Asiatic deity, identified by the Egyptians with Ḥathor, as a goddess of love.

RĀ (Rē‘), god.
Man with the head of a falcon surmounted by the solar-disc and *uraeus*-serpent ⚬. Cult-centre : Heliopolis. Represents the sun in the fullness of his strength. The most frequent form of the Sun-god. pp. 5 ff., 99 ff., and *passim*.

RENENŪTET (Ernutet), goddess.
(*a*) Woman, sometimes with the head of an *uraeus*-serpent ; (*b*) a large *uraeus*-serpent wearing